THE POOL OF BETHESDA

THE POOL OF BETHESDA

by Allan Cubitt

Warner Chappell Plays

LONDON

A Time Warner Company

First published in 1992
by Warner Chappell Plays Ltd
129 Park Street, London W1Y 3FA

ISBN 0 85676 156 7

Cover designed by Helen Lannaghan.
Printed by Commercial Colour Press, London E7.

FOR CLARE

THE POOL OF BETHESDA was first presented at the Orange Tree Theatre, Richmond on 5 September, 1991, with the following cast:

DR DANIEL PEARCE	Mick Ford
JANE	Maggie O'Neill
RUTH	Julia Ford
KATE	Katharine Rogers
HOGARTH/SIMON	Daniel Webb
MAID/SALLY	Rachel Clarke
FIGG/PATIENT/1ST DOCTOR	Ian Mercer
FANCY	Michael Haighton
18TH C. DOCTOR/2ND DOCTOR	Patrick John-Anthony
THE SICK	Members of the Company

Directed by Susan Hogg
Designed by Michael Vale
Music by Bill Crow
Lighting by Dickon O'Mara

An earlier version of THE POOL OF BETHESDA, directed by the author was staged at the Guildhall School of Music and Drama, winning the Thames TV Best Play and Best Production awards for 1990.

William Hogarth's canvas, *The Pool of Bethesda* (1735-36) still hangs on the Great Staircase at Saint Bartholomew's Hospital, Smithfields. James Figg was England's first Heavyweight Champion Boxer but, although Hogarth painted his portrait, there is no evidence to suggest that he appeared in *The Pool of Bethesda*. That, like the rest of the characters and the story, is part of the author's invention.

PROLOGUE

Three women, JANE, RUTH *and* KATE *occupy the stage.*
Light comes up on DANNY PEARCE'S *widow,* JANE. *She is an*
attractive woman in her late twenties. She has a small bunch
of red roses. The women do not talk to each other, each
existing in a separate space.

JANE   Oh, Danny.
                You're a bastard. To leave me like that.
                A widow at twenty-nine.
                A year. One year.
                It seems like yesterday.

                (*Light comes up on* PEARCE'S *sister,* RUTH.
                She carries a small bunch of garden-grown
                flowers.)

RUTH   It seems a lifetime ago . . .

JANE   I still feel so afraid.
                It'll be good to see Ruth.
                We said we'd meet today, your deathday.
                A year.
                And Kate. I wonder if Kate will be there?

                (*Light comes up on* KATE. *She's in her early*
                thirties and is dressed for work. KATE *is a*
                Senior Registrar in Neurosurgery at Saint
                Bartholomew's Hospital, London.)

KATE   This ward. This hospital. One year.
                I watched them, after he died. His wife, his
                sister. They looked as if they were behind
                glass. Like fish in a tank. Their mouths
                opened and closed silently. My white coat felt
                crisp with starch and I knew that if I moved it
                would break the silence in the room like a
                scream.

RUTH   I tried to go back as if nothing had happened,
                back to my husband, my daughter, waiting for
                the phone to ring, praying for the next job.

JANE   Sometimes I hated Ruth. When I felt her
                pushing me to the sides of my own sorrow,
                judging me.
                Little sister taking over.

RUTH   By Easter I couldn't stand it anymore.
                Friends of the Earth have a place in Kerry,
                the most westerly point in Ireland, the most
                westerly point in Europe. Just a peasant's
                cottage really but equipped with machines for
                measuring the pollution in the atmosphere. I
                went there Danny. I didn't want to see
                anyone, talk to anyone. It's the most difficult
                thing being alone . . .

JANE   I still see you. Sitting in the chair watching
                me.
                Standing in the bedroom. Not in a dream but
                actually there.

RUTH   Sometimes I felt I was losing myself. But I
                read, wrote. Beneath the mountains, beside
                the ocean I began to understand what you
                were telling me.
                That you need a relationship with yourself
                before you can have a relationship with
                others. After a while I began to quite like
                myself again . . .

                (RUTH goes.)

JANE   I have taken a lover on occasions.
                But always, during those hours before dawn,
                I've listened to the rhythm of his breathing,
                and when I've stretched out my hand have
                known it was your heart that I felt beating
                beneath the chest where my palm rested.

KATE   This ward, this hospital. A year ago. Doctor
                Daniel Pearce.
                Male, aged thirty-five years, three months:
                headaches; epilepsy; papilloedema; terminal
                attacks of opisthotonos . . .
                I don't think I can go today, too much work to
                do.

(KATE *goes. A man enters. The man they've
been talking about. He is* DANIEL PEARCE,
*thirty-five, casually dressed in modern
clothes. He stands at the centre of the stage.
He appears to be staring at something.* JANE
addresses him.)

JANE   A touch of flu you said and I went off and
              phoned my lover. Oh God, I had no idea you
              were so ill. What was it Kate told me?
              Tumours of the temporal lobe may cause
              psychic seizures. Dreams. Visions.
              I had no idea when I saw you that day staring
              at the painting on the Great Stairway.
              No idea what was happening inside your poor
              head . . .

              (JANE *goes. Only* PEARCE *remains as the
              lights change. A figure steps out of the
              shadows towards him. He wears 18th-century
              dress and carries a sketch book. He is a squat
              man of thirty-eight with short cropped hair
              beneath his cap. They face each other.*)

PEARCE   Hogarth?

              (HOGARTH *smiles.*)

ACT ONE

Music. The lighting change is complete. Suddenly PEARCE *is
addressing the gallery of an 18th-century operating theatre.*
HOGARTH *starts sketching.* PEARCE'S *assistants, dressed like
18th-century doctors, join him. One carries* PEARCE'S
trepanning set.

PEARCE   Gentlemen. So far I have demonstrated the
              art of blood-letting, and the encouragement of
              the issuing of poisons by means of, one: cuts
              artificially kept open; two: seatons - the
              insertion of threads under the skin - and
              three: blisters, produced by hot irons or
              caustics.

(HOGARTH'S *chalk sounds on the paper as he makes a sketch of* PEARCE.)

PEARCE   Today I can promise you something of great interest.

           (*The patient is dragged forward. He seems drunk. They sit him in a chair.* PEARCE *stands behind him.* HOGARTH *sketches the operation.*)

PEARCE   A fellow with a cancerous tumour in the brain.
           The skull is a rigid globe that will not permit any expansion from within.
           Unless we can reduce the pressure that the growth is creating inside the cranium he is sure to collapse and die.
           Even now, the pain is such that, unless completely doped with opium, he is, to all intents and purposes, demented.
           Can we save the poor soul from bedlam?
           Trepanning is his only hope.
           Pay close attention.

           (PEARCE *instructs his assistants with a sudden urgency and authority.*)

PEARCE   Give him the leather to bite on.
           Lay firm hold of his limbs.

           (*They hold the patient.* PEARCE *takes up a knife.*)

PEARCE   First, cut a triangular flap of scalp that we can peel back to expose the skull.

           (*A struggle.* HOGARTH *has stopped sketching to watch, horrified.*)

PEARCE   Hold him firmly. Hold him!
           Secondly, with the drill . . .

           (*As* PEARCE *takes up his drill, which looks like a sturdy corkscrew with an inch-wide*

circular bit, there is a cry and a crash.
HOGARTH *has dropped his sketchbook.*
PEARCE *pauses.*)

PEARCE   Are you all right, Sir?

HOGARTH   Perfectly.

PEARCE   Shall I proceed?

HOGARTH   By all means.

             (HOGARTH *picks up the sketchbook.*)

PEARCE   Take out a small circle of bone . . .

             (PEARCE *starts to screw into the patient's
             skull. The patient screams.* HOGARTH *cries
             out. As he does so, all the figures except*
             HOGARTH *leave the stage.* HOGARTH *is
             doubled up. Perhaps he's been sick. The
             light grows, opens out. A* SERVANT *brings two
             glasses and a bottle.* HOGARTH *fortifies
             himself with copious draughts of liquor. After
             a while, he is joined by* PEARCE.)

PEARCE   I didn't see you leave. Did you make your
             sketch?

HOGARTH   Another time.
             Feel embarrassed . . .

PEARCE   You shouldn't.

HOGARTH   An artist should be able to look upon any
             sight.

PEARCE   Some sights must remain too much surely?

HOGARTH   What sight is too much for the surgeon I
             wonder?

PEARCE   The sight of his own blood.

HOGARTH   Of course. Drink?

PEARCE   I drink nothing but water, Sir.

HOGARTH   Yes.

                  (HOGARTH *pours himself a huge glass and
                  swigs it down.*)

HOGARTH   Isn't this splendid? The Great Hall!
                  Soon the walls will be covered with the names
                  of benefactors. And a lot of inferior portraits.
                  People who give to charity so like their
                  names to be mentioned somewhere don't
                  they? Nothing vulgar but recognition all the
                  same.
                  So vast and splendid.
                  Doesn't it make you want to drop your
                  breeches and shit in the corner?

                  (PEARCE *waits patiently.* HOGARTH *dismisses
                  the servant.*)

HOGARTH   Excuse me but you have blood on your
                  cheek.

                  (PEARCE *wipes it away automatically.*)

                  Perhaps you have heard that there are plans
                  to decorate the walls of the Great Stairway
                  with paintings?

PEARCE   Where?

HOGARTH   Where? Here, Saint Bartholomew's.

PEARCE   Oh yes.

HOGARTH   Perhaps you've also heard that there is talk
                  of commissioning a wop dauber to complete
                  the work? One Jacopo Amigoni?

PEARCE   No . . .

HOGARTH   I intend to get that commission.

PEARCE   How?

HOGARTH	I'll paint the buggers for nothing.
PEARCE	. . . ?
HOGARTH	Bear the cost of the work myself.
PEARCE	Why?
HOGARTH	Why? To stop the Italian Monkey getting the credit.
PEARCE	Oh, I see.
HOGARTH	Not just that. And to prove that a British painter can handle such subjects. What the puffers in books call the grand business of History painting. Two massive canvases - the English damp makes wop fresco useless - Biblical in theme. The first: The Pool of Bethesda.

(HOGARTH *takes a screwed-up piece of paper from his pocket and reads.*)

"Now there is at Jerusalem, by the sheep market a pool which is called in the Hebrew tongue Bethesda, having five porches.
In these lay a great multitude of impotent folk, of blind, of halt, withered, waiting for the moving of the water . . .
Whosoever then first after the troubling of the water stepped in was made whole of whatsoever disease he had . . .
The lame man . . . " etc, etc, "Jesus saith unto him . . . 'Rise, take up thy bed and walk.' And immediately, the man was made whole, and took up his bed . . . " so on and so forth.

(*He hands* PEARCE *the piece of paper.*)

PEARCE	I'm still at a loss to see how this concerns me.
HOGARTH	I want you to help me.
PEARCE	To secure the commission?

HOGARTH   In a way.

PEARCE   How?

HOGARTH   Once the task is mine I intend to do what no
               wop dauber would do.

               (HOGARTH *seems genuinely enthusiastic about
               the project.*)

               My pictures are my stage and my men and
               women my players.
               You can help me find the impotent folk in the
               hospital.
               The blind, the halt, the withered.
               I'll put 'em in the thing. Seven feet high.

               (*Pause.*)

               Take me on your rounds. We'll find them
               together.

PEARCE   A man of your prestige can walk the wards at
               will. Not a day goes by without a party of
               well-to-do gawpers visiting the hospital,
               wishing to have their own good health
               confirmed by the infirmity of others.
               Wandering the wards, scented handkerchiefs
               at their nostrils.

HOGARTH   I want you as my guide. Doctor Pearce, the
               majority of your brethren are Charlatans -
               worse. Butchers. You are different.

PEARCE   I can think of no excuse that will allow me to
               say 'No' to a Governor of my hospital.

HOGARTH   Good.

               (PEARCE *is about to bid* HOGARTH *farewell.*)

               There's something more.

               (*Beat.*)

               I want you to model for Christ.

PEARCE   I beg your pardon?

HOGARTH   I need a Christ. I think it should be you.

PEARCE   I don't . . .

HOGARTH   In "The Pool of Bethesda."

(PEARCE *is taken aback*.)

PEARCE   Why me?

HOGARTH   I saw you, some time ago, heal a young girl. A young girl in a blue dress. She had a lump here, on her wrist. You pressed and kneaded and little by little, the growth went away . . .

PEARCE   Perhaps your choice of subjects is fitting. Too many people see our hospital as a place of death. I applaud your desire to represent it as a place of hope, of healing. But it is not a place of miracles, Mr Hogarth, where the maimed can be make whole, regardless of what ails them. What you saw could have been achieved by hitting it with the family bible. Nothing miraculous.

HOGARTH   It wasn't what you did, it was the way you did it . . .

PEARCE   You saw me in the cutting-room just now. I could do nothing for the poor fellow. I hope, for his sake, that death comes swiftly. I'm no miracle-worker, Mr Hogarth. Excuse me . . .

HOGARTH   The story works as a simile Doctor, not as a factual account in a newspaper. I am a commentator on human, not divine behaviour. My object is drastic and my aim to draw tears from the spectator.

PEARCE   And who will that be, Sir? On the Great Stairway?
Not the patients to be sure.

HOGARTH   Governors and most importantly, potential
               donors upon whose charity the hospital
               depends.
               Rich merchants, they are our masters now.
               What draws me to the story? The man who
               has no servant to put him in the pool, whose
               place is taken by another.
               If I use, as models, patients from these wards,
               it will seem real enough to you.

PEARCE   Perhaps.

HOGARTH   Don't underestimate me, Sir. My 'Harlot's
               Progress' made me a small fortune. I will
               make you immortal.
               Think about it. I will haunt you Doctor
               Pearce until I get my way.

               (*The interview is over.* PEARCE *is about to
               leave when three women burst in. They are*
               JANE, RUTH *and* KATE. *They are the women
               from the Prologue, but now, in* PEARCE'S
               *dream, they assume different characters of his
               creation and inhabit this Hogarthian world.*
               KATE, *who is dressed in the height of fashion,
               and* RUTH, *an equally fashionable young
               actress, are both eager to appear in*
               HOGARTH'S *new painting.* JANE - *who is
               dressed more modestly - is more aloof and
               watchful. They approach the two men.*)

KATE   Billy! You elusive boy. We've searched
               everywhere for you.

HOGARTH   I do believe it's a party of well-to-do gawpers . . .

JANE   We've been visiting the wards.

RUTH   Such fun, so many amusing characters . . .

KATE   We had to find you as soon as we heard.

HOGARTH   Heard what?

RUTH   That you are planning a new canvas.

JANE   We're curious to know the subject, Mister
                Hogarth.

HOGARTH   Christ healing the sick at the Pool of
                Bethesda.

JANE   I see.

KATE   Will you be working here?

HOGARTH   No. At a studio in Covent Garden.

RUTH   Covent Garden. Excellent.

                (*Since her entrance*, PEARCE *has been staring
                at* JANE. *Anxious to be introduced, he clears
                his throat noisily.*)

HOGARTH   I'm sorry Doctor. Ladies. Allow me to present
                Doctor Daniel Pearce, Assistant Surgeon and
                Lithotomist here at Saint Bartholomew's.
                Mistress Katharine Wood . . .

KATE   Surgeon you say. I hate hospitals. Visiting
                those wards has thoroughly depressed my
                spirits.

HOGARTH   Mistress Jones, one of our most celebrated
                young actresses. And Mistress Long.

PEARCE   Jane. Such beautiful eyes.
                Those eyes . . .

HOGARTH   Doctor Pearce has just agreed to model as
                Christ.

KATE   Really?

                (*They all move towards him, fascinated.*)

PEARCE   Well . . .

RUTH   How exciting.

JANE   What an honour.

                (JANE *looks at* PEARCE *and smiles, a gentle,
                radiant smile.* PEARCE'S *eyes do not leave that
                direction for the rest of the scene.*)

PEARCE   Yes.

                (HOGARTH *has his Christ.*)

HOGARTH   Good.

                (*They drift away. The light reduces until*
                PEARCE *seems alone on stage.*)

PEARCE   Jane, I'll remember the first time I saw you . . .
                Your eyes, so clear, I'll remember always . . .

                (*A huge half-naked man is approaching*
                PEARCE *out of the darkness. He is* FIGG,
                England's champion boxer. He grabs
                PEARCE'S *head in his huge hands, crushing it.*
                PEARCE *cries out in pain.*)

FIGG   I'll tear your head off and eat your brains for
                breakfast . . .

                (*And with that he butts* PEARCE'S *head and
                roars with laughter.* PEARCE *collapses in pain.
                The light grows. We are in the Covent
                Garden studio.* HOGARTH *is busying himself
                with preparations for his first studies for the
                painting.*)

PEARCE   Crush my head like that again and it will split
                like a coconut at a Shy.

FIGG   That was nothing, Doctor. Compared to one
                of my bothering blows that was a caress, a
                fondle.

(FIGG *hauls* PEARCE *up, instructing him as he does so.*)

Now, stand squarely on, Doctor so you might lead off with either hand.

HOGARTH   I'm afraid Figg considers it his bounden duty to instruct all Gentlemen in the manly arts. I myself have sparred with him and my advice to you is 'ware his right . . .

FIGG   Good. Good. Look into my eyes, don't watch my fists.

(*They spar.*)

HOGARTH   His right. Doctor.

(FIGG *has landed the punch.* PEARCE *cries out.*)

HOGARTH   That's the one.

(KATE, RUTH *and* JANE *arrive.*)

KATE   Boxing!

RUTH   How brave Doctor, to face the mighty Figg.

(KATE *runs her hand over* FIGG'S *bare torso.*)

KATE   Mmmm, the champion of all England.

JANE   Take care, Doctor Pearce.

(*They make an eager audience for the boxing.* PEARCE *is anxious to impress* JANE. *Both men are now showing off for the women. They spar.* FIGG *bulls him.* PEARCE *slips under his arm and away to safety.*)

FIGG   Were you taught those pretty steps by your Dancing Master?

PEARCE   Nimble, eh?

                  (FIGG *lunges again but* PEARCE, *in a move
                  owing more to Mohammed Ali than the bare
                  knuckleman, slips the blow. His arms drop to
                  his side and he dances around.* HOGARTH *is
                  drawing, loving it.* FIGG *is angry.*)

FIGG   Confound your prancing, Sir!

                  (FIGG *advances.* PEARCE *is almost running
                  away.*)

FIGG   Are you mocking me? You son of a whore.

HOGARTH   Come on James, it's just a little sport.

FIGG   Mock me Doctor and I will kill you.

                  (*Suddenly the match has turned ugly.* FIGG *is
                  determined now.* PEARCE *proves brave. He
                  lands some blows on* FIGG *who is biding his
                  time.*)

HOGARTH   Don't let him grab you, Doctor. His grip is
                  like a vice.

                  (*Suddenly* FIGG *shows what he can do. He
                  grabs* PEARCE, *getting him in a headlock.*
                  PEARCE *cries out in pain. The others try to
                  intervene.*)

RUTH   Stop it, you great brute.

HOGARTH   Let him go, Figg!

JANE   You're killing him. Do something.

                  (*Between them they manage to haul* FIGG *off.
                  Released,* PEARCE *collapses.*)

RUTH   Figg! Look what you've done.

(RUTH, KATE *and* JANE *set about ministering to* PEARCE.)

FIGG   I won't be mocked.

PEARCE   My head, my head.

JANE   Here, let me help you.

PEARCE   There are tears in your eyes.

JANE   I can't bear to see you in pain.
I can't bear it . . .

HOGARTH   Figg. As a punishment for nearly killing my Christ, I shall do what no opponent in the ring has ever done: lay you out. You shall be the man who has lain infirm for eight-and-thirty years.

FIGG   The keeper of the pool, you said.

(HOGARTH *fetches a big pillow and bandages.*)

HOGARTH   The lame man, or you won't be paid. Down, Sir.

(FIGG, *angry and unhappy now, sits on his bed. He drapes himself with a few pieces of bandage.* HOGARTH *fetches some lengths of red and blue cloth.*)

Now ladies, if you will be of assistance. Undress the Doctor and put these on him.

(HOGARTH *hands them the cloths.*)

* * * *

HOGARTH   His robes.

(*Music as the lights go down until only* PEARCE *and the three women,* RUTH, KATE

and JANE *are really visible. The three
women start to remove* PEARCE'S *shirt and
dress him in his robes. Their voices are soft,
caressing, sincere.*)

JANE   Such soft flesh.

ALL   Soon be slack.

KATE   Such smooth skin.

ALL   Soon be wrinkled.

RUTH   Such firm limbs.

ALL   Soon be withered.

KATE   Such a warm colour.

ALL   Soon be pale.

RUTH   Such hot breath.

ALL   Soon be smothered.

JANE   Such a beating heart.

ALL   Soon be stilled.

            (*They've draped him in the red and blue
            robes of Christ. The music stops.*)

                        * * * *

HOGARTH   Excellent, excellent. Here.

            (*He stands* PEARCE *ready to approach the
            prostrate* FIGG. *The three women stand or sit
            to one side.*)

FIGG   I won't be mocked.

HOGARTH   That's enough Figg. Here, Doctor.

(HOGARTH *positions* PEARCE *and looks at the picture he has created.*)

HOGARTH   I thought you were taller.

PEARCE   What?

HOGARTH   The lame man must be raised from a height. Here, as you approach him, stand on this.

(*He places a box for* PEARCE *to stand on. He gives them their lines.* KATE, JANE *and* RUTH *are watching.*)

HOGARTH   Wilt thou be made whole?

PEARCE   What?

HOGARTH   These are your lines.

PEARCE   Oh.

HOGARTH   Repeat them. Wilt thou be made whole.

PEARCE   Wilt thou be made whole?

KATE   It's like being at the play!

RUTH   Like no performance I've ever given . . .

HOGARTH   Ladies, please. Leave us now. We have work to do.

KATE   Then we'll have to find more amusing company.

HOGARTH   Come back tomorrow.

PEARCE   Yes, do . . .

JANE   We will.

KATE   There's romance in the air!

(*The three women withdraw.*)

HOGARTH   Sir, I have no man, when the water is
               troubled, to put me into the pool.

PEARCE   Sir I have no man . . .

HOGARTH   Figg!

FIGG   Sir, I have no man, when the . . .

HOGARTH   The water is troubled . . .

FIGG   . . . water is troubled, to put me into the pool.

HOGARTH   But while I am coming another steppeth down
               before me.

FIGG   But while I am coming another steppeth down
               before me.

HOGARTH   Rise, take up thy bed and walk.

PEARCE   Yes.

               (*Music gently underscores the following.*
               HOGARTH *goes to his sketchbook, takes up
               black chalk to sketch. A lighting change. Just*
               PEARCE *and* FIGG *in dramatic light. This time
               as if it is real,* PEARCE *approaches* FIGG
               *slowly. He mounts the boxes and stands over
               him. There is great compassion in the scene.*
               HOGARTH *is struck by its potency.*)

PEARCE   How long have you lain infirm?

FIGG   A long time, Master.

PEARCE   How long?

FIGG   Thirty-and-eight years.

PEARCE   Wilt thou be made whole?

FIGG   Sir, I have no man, when the water is
               troubled, to put me into the pool: but while I
               am coming another steppeth down before me.

PEARCE   Rise, take up thy bed and walk.

                  (*And in saying that,* PEARCE *adopts the pose
                  from the painting, right hand on hip, left held
                  out, palm upwards, indicating* FIGG *should try
                  to rise.* HOGARTH *captures the moment.*)

HOGARTH   Yes. That's it. That's it.

                          * * * *

                  (*The light reduces until only* PEARCE *is
                  visible. Strange subterranean sounds, water
                  rushing, dripping.*)

PEARCE   My head, my head . . .
                  Those punches . . .
                  Hurts so . . .
                  That headlock . . .
                  If I move . . .

                  (*He moves his head from side to side, like the
                  beginnings of a fit.*)

                  Feels like water rushing . . .
                  Sounds like water rushing.

                  (*Voices are coming from somewhere.* KATE
                  and her MAID *are talking to* HOGARTH.)

MAID   Then in the summer Madam'll take the waters
                  in Bath again.

KATE   Where, no doubt, I sh'll be fleeced of a small
                  fortune.
MAID   And meet the handsome French gentleman
                  again, perhaps?

                  (PEARCE *steps down from his box as the lights
                  return to normal.* FIGG *is there. The others
                  start to arrive.*)

MAID   Oh Mister Hogarth, he had the prettiest
            manners and way of speaking that you've
            ever heard.

HOGARTH   Monkey jabber! Mincing, dancing, prancing
            monkeys. As it is your happiness, young lady,
            to be born a Briton, let it also be your boast.

            (*Clearly* HOGARTH *is trying to press ahead
            with the canvas and is grouping the figures
            on the right hand side of his composition.*
            KATE, *now wrapped in a diaphanous sheet,
            sits with her* MAID *waiting to be placed.* FIGG
            is rigging up a swing from the studio roof.
            PEARCE *tries to focus on them.*)

FIGG   Ruth can perch on this . . .

HOGARTH   Perch? She's not a Goldfinch, she's the
            archangel Raphael.

PEARCE   I thought you were planning to show the
            suffering at the poolside.

            (RUTH *emerges. She is wearing a set of wings
            - she is the angel who will trouble the
            waters.*)

RUTH   I suffer Doctor. These wings must weigh
            forty pounds.

PEARCE   Weeks of sketches. Where are the sick, the
            infirm?

HOGARTH   All in good time. The left hand side of the
            canvas shall be reserved for the common
            folk. My aim is to satisfy all tastes.
FANCY   At the expense of artistic wholeness . . .

            (SIR JOHN FANCY, *the inevitable dandy, has
            entered. At first* PEARCE *doesn't notice he is
            with* JANE.)

FANCY   You are the talk of the town once again,
            Billy.

HOGARTH   Sir John.

                 (FIGG *is helping* RUTH *onto the swing. She is laughing and giggling.* PEARCE *watches.*)

FANCY   Covent Garden is a-buzz with tales of history painting in the grand manner. So here I am, Doubting Thomas style, to see for myself.

                 (FANCY *is looking around.*)

                 Bearded lady? Must see. Women giving birth to rabbits? Must see. Twins joined at the head. Must see. Hogarth giving up his miserable graver for the heroic brush . . . ?

HOGARTH   Yes, yes, yes.

FANCY   Come on, Bill, that's more canvas than you've ever tried to fill before. Find space for Janey and me.

HOGARTH   Jane, of course . . .

PEARCE   Why, is she here with him?

KATE   Sir John and Jane are lovers, Doctor. Didn't you know?

PEARCE   No . . .

KATE   I thought everyone in London knew.

FANCY   The subject eludes me - is it Christ's tea-party?

HOGARTH   Christ healing the sick.

FANCY   Bravo.

PEARCE   But there are no sick. There's nothing wrong with any of these people.
                 Figg doesn't look lame. Why has he got a bandage round his head?

(HOGARTH *looks at* JANE.)

HOGARTH   Why bring that up now? You've spent weeks
               raising him and you bring that up now. Figg,
               why have you got a bandage round your
               head?

FIGG   I don't know.

PEARCE   Look at him. He's as strong as an ox.

HOGARTH   Well it's too late now.
               Here. Kate on the stretcher, attended by your
               Maid. That's it. Splendid.

               (HOGARTH *creates a sick baby from a bundle
               of rags. He gives it to* JANE.)

               Your baby, my dear.

JANE   What ails the child?

HOGARTH   She has been born with the pox.

               (JANE *cradles the rags like a child in her
               arms.*)

               And Sir John. You are the keeper of the pool.
               You are holding back this unfortunate woman
               with her sick baby, while taking a bribe from
               Kate's Maid.

FANCY   The keeper you say?

HOGARTH   Yes.

FANCY   Is he quite central to the composition?

HOGARTH   Quite central.

               (*He positions them, including* RUTH *as an
               angel suspended from the ceiling, and* FIGG
               as the lame man. KATE *is seated as if on a
               stretcher waiting to be carried into the pool,*

(FANCY - *as the keeper - pushes* JANE *and her baby away while accepting money as a bribe from* KATE'S MAID. PEARCE *is on his box.* HOGARTH *starts sketching. After a moment* PEARCE *addresses him.*)

PEARCE   You said to me, the blind, the halt, the withered.

HOGARTH   I'll come to the hospital, do sketches. The whole left hand side of the canvas as you look at it will be for them.

(PEARCE *comes down from his box to talk to* HOGARTH.)

PEARCE   But these people shouldn't be there at all. It's Jerusalem, not Covent Garden. It's by a sheep market, not the opera!

(HOGARTH *stops work to argue.* FIGG, *bored, wanders up to* RUTH *on the swing. He pushes her on it.*)

HOGARTH   Do not the rich and famous get sick? Do they not suffer? Are they not made of flesh and blood? Is not their tenement of clay as frail as your Watchman, Sweep, Lighterman, your Billingsgate woman?

PEARCE   In a word? No.
Of course wealth cannot eliminate disease but it can help prevent it. It can ensure the best treatment.

(PEARCE'S *appeal is being undermined somewhat by the noise* RUTH *is making.*)

RUTH   No . . . Figg, stop it . . .

PEARCE   A warm room . . .

RUTH   No . . . stop it . . .

PEARCE   . . . a clean bed to die in.

RUTH   Feel . . .

PEARCE   It can mean good fresh food to eat, clean
              linen.

RUTH   I'm gonna be . . .

PEARCE   Servants to fetch and carry . . .

              (RUTH *is sick. Uproar. The composition
              breaks up as* RUTH *swings back and forth in
              the air.*)

HOGARTH   For Christ's sake . . .

RUTH   I told you, you bastard.

HOGARTH   Stay where you are! Stay where you are!
              Jesus. This is not a game. Positions! Doctor
              please.

PEARCE   No, I'm sorry but this is all wrong. The pool,
              the pool must be . . .

              (*They wait.* PEARCE *is suffering. His head
              hurts, his thoughts are confused.*)

PEARCE   It must be. It should be . . .

HOGARTH   It might be. If you gave me a chance it might
              be.

PEARCE   No! Something . . . other . . .

HOGARTH   What?

PEARCE   I don't know what it should be . . .

HOGARTH   Thank you Doctor.

PEARCE   But it should not be this. These people . . .
              They know nothing of the world. They never
              venture beyond their elegant squares. If they
              were to walk through laystalls and bawdy

houses, the pawnbrokers, gin-shops, ale-
houses and see . . .
Amongst the beggars and shed-dwellers . . .
So much filth and rags and misery . . .

(*They stare at him. He's in tears. He peters
out.*)

HOGARTH   You think I don't know that? This is my city
               too. Look at my drawings. Good God, I grew
               up within the walls of the Fleet Prison where
               my father was incarcerated for debt.

PEARCE   When epidemics threaten this lot flee from
               the town.

HOGARTH   What should they do? Stay and be infected?

               (PEARCE *is floundering. He doesn't know
               what to say.*)

PEARCE   Damn you. You'll learn, you'll soon learn
               what it's like to be in constant pain, in fear for
               your very lives.

               (*All but* HOGARTH *laugh derisively.* PEARCE
               grabs JANE *pulls her round.*)

               Why are you here with him?

JANE   Let go of me.

PEARCE   You're no part of these people.

               (PEARCE *holds her, claiming her. His hand
               finds her breast. At first she seems to want
               him, her breath shallow, excited.*)

               I can see it in your eyes, the way you look at
               the baby in your arms . . .

               (*But now it seems as if an electric charge is
               travelling down his arm, wounding her in the*

breast. The pleasure has turned to pain, real
pain. JANE *tries to remove his hand.*)

JANE   You're hurting me.

PEARCE   Why are you always running from me, Jane?

JANE   Why do you want to hurt me, Danny?

PEARCE   You're not like them.

JANE   Why do you want to hurt me?

PEARCE   Why are you here with him?

JANE   Let me go. Your touch is painful to me. You
              don't touch me anymore . . .

              (*She struggles free, clutching her breast in*
              pain, dropping the bundle of rags as she runs
              out.)

                              * * * *

              (*The Healthy* - FANCY, FIGG, KATE *and her*
              MAID - *aim their comments at* PEARCE.)

FANCY   My nerves are highly strung. I feel much
              more acutely than the common herd . . .

KATE   The lower orders do not feel refined pain . . .

RUTH   The poor get the diseases they deserve.
              Too much cheap gin, too much laudanum . . .

FIGG   Why not take pride in the flesh?

KATE   A full bosom, a well-rounded belly are signs
              of good breeding.

FANCY   Now there are charity hospitals will not the
              poor take to shamming sickness . . . ?

KATE   To exploit us and gain food, shelter, a bed?

PEARCE   Listen to this . . .

HOGARTH   Yes, perfect aren't they?

PEARCE   For what?

HOGARTH   For those people who will not allow the lame
                man into the pool because he has no servant
                to help him? Who take the places of the truly
                ill because they can pay for their treatment.

                (*Silence.* PEARCE *sees* HOGARTH'S *reasoning.
                The Healthy withdraw.*)

                I told you not to underestimate me, Sir.

PEARCE   But you still need the sick. Come to the
                hospital. Come with me on my rounds.

                (PEARCE *removes his robes.*)

HOGARTH   All right.

PEARCE   Come with me now.

HOGARTH   All right.

                (*A cello starts to play.* PEARCE *listens for a
                moment. The lights change. We are in Saint
                Bartholomew's Hospital. It is dark and dank.*
                HOGARTH *is unsettled. He looks around him,
                taking it in. This is* PEARCE'S *world.*)

PEARCE   Choose as you like Sir. There are many more
                from whence they came.

HOGARTH   The smell.

PEARCE   How can you doubt the significance of
                poverty on our Nation's health?

HOGARTH   I . . .

PEARCE   Look around you: walls and ceiling a dingy
                brown that does not show dirt; wooden floor,

wooden beds, harbouring vermin of all sorts; mattresses sodden; linen stained; the wound dresser spreading infection with his dirty bucket, his soiled bandages. Here.

HOGARTH   What is it?

PEARCE   The top of my cane contains lemon juice. Breathe deeply.

(HOGARTH *takes the cane and smells gratefully.*)

PEARCE   The smallpox and deadly fevers should be avoided, but we have a ocean of eruptions, swellings, scrofula, wasting conditions to choose from.

HOGARTH   Why so angry Doctor?

PEARCE   That last time at your studio? The suggestion that you get the disease you deserve? There Sir, a baby, blighted from birth. Congenital syphilis. Come, approach them. Beneath their bandages, their disfigurements, they are our fellows.

(*Little by little The Sick have begun to move forward out of the shadows. They are the figures who appear in* HOGARTH'S *canvas, "The Pool of Bethesda".*)

HOGARTH   What is your name?

WOMAN   The sick have no names.

(PEARCE *introduces them to the painter.*)

PEARCE   She has an abscess on her breast.

WOMAN   We leave our names at the door.

(*The next is the Man With Gout. His hand is bandaged and in a sling.*)

MAN WITH GOUT	And put on a robe of fear.
PEARCE	He has gout.
WOMAN	For now we must be patient.
MAN WITH GOUT	Ask no questions.
PEARCE	(*referring to the wild-eyed woman with her head covered*) Acute melancholia.
MELANCHOLIC	We are the forgotten for we wear the face of death.
MAN WITH GOUT	Forget your family.
MELANCHOLIC	Forget your friends. For they will abandon you.
BLIND MAN	Who can blame them?
PEARCE	(*referring to the Blind Man with his staff*) Total eclipse, no sun, no moon.
BLIND MAN	No one will remember you.
	(HOGARTH *helps them move forward now.*)
HOGARTH	Can you have faith any more?
WOMAN	Faith is hard. No one can share your pain.
HOGARTH	Do you have hope? Tell me you're still hopeful! There is nothing without hope!
BLIND MAN	Perhaps there is hope.
HOGARTH	There must be.

(PEARCE *sees that* JANE *has joined the Chorus of The Sick, who murmur their prayer together.*)

THE SICK   Praying every day for a miracle.
               Praying . . .

PEARCE   Why are you here?

THE SICK   Praying every day for a miracle.
               Every day . . .

PEARCE   What's wrong?

JANE   You know that better than anyone.

PEARCE   I? How do I know? I haven't examined you.

JANE   You don't need to.

PEARCE   Why?

JANE   Because I am your creation.

PEARCE   Do you have a fever?

               (*He tries to touch her brow.*)

JANE   Don't touch me . . .

THE SICK   Praying every day for a miracle.
               A miracle . . .

PEARCE   No. I won't be blamed.

               (HOGARTH *hands* JANE *the bundle of rags which she treats as if it were her baby. The light changes as* HOGARTH *positions The Sick and sketches them.* RUTH, *dressed as the angel and* FIGG *have taken up their positions.*)

PEARCE   I've always done my best.

I wash my hands of this guilt, I've done all I
can.
I told you, I'm a doctor, not a miracle-worker.

(HOGARTH *approaches* PEARCE.)

HOGARTH   Come on Doctor. You wanted it like this.
               Your robes if you please.

PEARCE   It's not my fault the lame man will never rise.
               It's you who chose that moment. For as long
               as this painting exists the lame man will never
               rise.

               (PEARCE *begins to put them on.* HOGARTH
               helps PEARCE *climb onto his box. During this
               argument* JANE *has become distressed.*)

JANE   I'm sorry, I have to go . . .

HOGARTH   What?

JANE   I don't feel well . . .

HOGARTH   Of course my dear . . .

JANE   I can't bear this . . .

               (JANE *hands* HOGARTH *the rags as if they
               were her child. He takes them in that spirit.
               When she's gone he allows them to drop
               open.* PEARCE *looks after her, concerned,
               agitated.*)

PEARCE   Why is she always running from me?

FIGG   Because she's running to the arms of her
               lover.

PEARCE   What?

FIGG   Her Johnny. Though if you're hot for her
               you've only to go to the Sun Inn, to see her
               again.

PEARCE   The Sun Inn?

FIGG   She performs postures there. Strips off her
              underthings and performs a series of postures
              over a silver salver.

PEARCE   No!

FIGG   For her finale, she extinguishes a lighted
              candle in her vagina . . .

PEARCE   Filthy, dirty . . .

HOGARTH   Keep still!

FIGG   Now how is that possible, Doctor?

PEARCE   Not her . . .

FIGG   Without injury?

RUTH   Take no notice Doctor, he's . . .

FIGG   Now, what is it they call her? Oh yes,
              Mistress Cunny, Fair Janey Sweet Cunt . . .

              (PEARCE *turns to* HOGARTH *for help.*)

PEARCE   You're not drawing him . . .

HOGARTH   What?

PEARCE   . . . there's no reason for him to be here.

              (HOGARTH *considers.*)

HOGARTH   Oh all right. At least then I might get some
              peace.

PEARCE   So, rise, take up thy bed and walk.

              (FIGG *plays up to this, to the initial amusement
              of* RUTH *and* HOGARTH. *There is a stirring in*

his legs. He starts to move. No one notices how The Sick are transfixed by this.)

PEARCE Go on, you bear-garden bruiser: rise, take up thy bed and bugger off.

(HOGARTH *and* RUTH *are laughing.* FIGG *plays up to his audience. He drags himself to his knees. He rubs his legs. The Sick break their poses and watch with increasing fascination.*)

PEARCE Behold, thou art made whole: sin no more lest a worse thing come unto thee.

(FIGG *walks. Now The Sick are beside themselves. They are witnessing a miracle.*)

THE SICK A miracle!
The lame man walks! The lame man walks!

PEARCE No. He can walk.

THE SICK Yes, a miracle.

PEARCE No, he could walk anyway.

(*But The Sick believe they've seen a miracle. They are shouting, crying, wailing.* PEARCE *is completely bewildered.*)

THE SICK I believe in you Doctor. Cure me, cure me!
I am old let me go first . . .

BLIND MAN I am blind - someone tell me what happened.

PEARCE Figg, Figg . . .

BLIND MAN What happened?

PEARCE . . . tell them.

THE SICK Yes, yes, tell us.

(*It's in* FIGG'S *hands now.*)

FIGG   I was lame, now I can walk!

RUTH   Figg you bastard! You utter bastard!

                              * * * *

                (*Music. Lights focus on* PEARCE *as The Sick
                overwhelm him, dragging him down beneath
                his robes.*)

THE SICK   Me. Me. Me. Me. Cure me. Cure me.

                (*They are stripping him, pulling wildly at his
                robes.*)

                Me! Heal me! Me! Heal me!

PEARCE   I can't heal you, I can't heal you . . .

                (*They've stripped him of his robes. They pull
                away from him leaving him prostrate at the
                centre of the stage.*)

                I can't heal you, I can't heal you . . .

                              * * * *

                (*The lights change as the music stops.* RUTH,
                *still dressed as the angel, approaches him.
                She stands over him.*)

PEARCE   Too many people. Look . . .
                Too many sick, too many ill . . .
                My mother . . . my father . . .
                So many dead.

RUTH   Yes.

PEARCE   Do you see them?

RUTH   No.

PEARCE   Your wings are strong and broad, you must
                trouble the waters . . .

RUTH   I can't stay. I must go.

PEARCE   Please don't leave me. Wrap me in your
              wings and never leave me.

RUTH   I have to leave you . . .

              (RUTH *goes.*)

PEARCE   I can't heal them all.

              (JANE *enters to him.*)

JANE   You can heal me. If you want to.

              (PEARCE *looks up, sees her there.*)

PEARCE   Go to your lover, to John. Leave me alone.

JANE   Your jealousy is not reason enough. Not for
              what you're doing to me.

PEARCE   What am I doing to you?

JANE   Why have you cursed me like this?

PEARCE   I haven't cursed you, I love you . . .

              (JANE *starts to unfasten her dress.* PEARCE
              *watches. She exposes her left breast to him.
              He cannot disguise his shock at finding it
              diseased.*)

JANE   I was whole until I came into your dream.
              This is your love . . .

PEARCE   What do you mean?

JANE   Your disease . . .

PEARCE   Mine? How can it be mine?

JANE   Because this is your world.
              I beg you, lift your curse from me, heal me . . .

PEARCE   We could operate, remove the breast . . .

JANE   Would that save me?

PEARCE   I don't know.

            (*She covers herself.*)

JANE   Would you leave me whole, unscarred?

PEARCE   Of course not . . .

JANE   No, you'd mutilate me . . .
            Just to save yourself. So you don't suffer.

PEARCE   No, that's not fair. I do care. I do still love
            you.

JANE   You don't love me any more.

PEARCE   Listen. Such beautiful music. One dance.

            (PEARCE *tries to take* JANE *in his arms. He
            holds her swaying to the music. She almost
            gives in to him but suddenly pushes him
            away.*)

JANE   No.

            (*She breaks away from him.*)

JANE   You can't fool me. I can feel you steeling
            yourself to take me in your arms as if a few
            moments of pity can compensate for this
            disease. The painting, the beautiful music,
            none of it helps at all . . .
            Not at all.

PEARCE   I do want you . . .

JANE   It's too late.

PEARCE   It's never too late.

(JANE *tries to leave. She finds her way blocked by* RUTH *and* KATE.)

* * * *

JANE   Let me pass.

KATE   Such soft flesh.

BOTH   Soon be food for the fishes.

RUTH   Such smooth skin.

BOTH   Soon be bloated.

KATE   Such firm limbs.

BOTH   Soon be withered.

RUTH   Such a warm colour.

BOTH   Soon be pale.

KATE   Such a beating heart . . .

BOTH   Soon be stilled.

KATE   Such hot breath.

BOTH   Soon be drowned.

JANE   Yes.

* * * *

(RUTH *goes, leaving* KATE. *As* PEARCE *moves towards* JANE *she intervenes.*)

KATE   Come Doctor. Don't give her another
              thought. I'll do anything you want. I'm not shy
              like her. There's nothing surprises me, I've
              seen it all. There's no part of the human body
              I haven't fingered. Tie me up if you want.
              Come in the sweat between my breasts. Look
              I've left my knickers off for you . . . I'm wet
              for you already.

PEARCE   No, I've never thought of you like that . . .

                (*She guides his hand beneath her skirt.*)

KATE   Your wedding ring finger. Slip it in. There.

PEARCE   I respect you . . .
                Ow! How do you do that?

KATE   Come Doctor, and I'll show you. Feel my
                body, feel my warmth, I'm alive, she's dead,
                come with me . . .

                (*With barely a glance at* JANE, PEARCE
                follows KATE *off.* JANE *stands for a moment,
                then she too leaves, defeated. After a
                moment,* PEARCE *stumbles back. He stands in
                the centre of the stage, moves his head from
                side to side.*)

PEARCE   The water swirls and rocks.
                Rocked on the water.
                Water dripping on rock.
                Wearing it down.
                My head is full of water. When I rock my
                head from side to side I can feel it rushing.
                I can hear it rushing . . .
                It's finished.

HOGARTH   And has been these two hundred and fifty-
                odd years.

                (HOGARTH *comes out of the shadows.*)

PEARCE   What?

HOGARTH   My canvas. "The Pool of Bethesda".

PEARCE   Yes. Yet you're still here.

HOGARTH   I hide in the shadows and listen.

PEARCE   What do people say?

HOGARTH   "One can almost smell their diseases."
          "Vivid, I grant you, but absurd in a painting
          in the Grand Style. The British have no grasp
          you see. It is the Italian Masters one should
          look to . . . "
          "Christ is a particular failure."
          "He looks like William Wollaston receiving
          guests in his drawing room."

PEARCE   I see.

HOGARTH   It is a failure. Awful painting. Worst I've ever
          done. Don't disagree will you. Miserable.
          Where are my holiday friends now? One
          whiff of failure and they desert you.

PEARCE   I won't desert you.

HOGARTH   Yes you will.

          (Pause.)

PEARCE   You know Jane is dead?

HOGARTH   No.

PEARCE   Drowned herself. Stones tied to her feet. Off
          Blackfriars Stairs.

HOGARTH   Oh God.

PEARCE   I told her of my love for her.

HOGARTH   What did she say?

PEARCE   She opened her blouse. Her left breast was
          rotten with cancer.

HOGARTH   And because of that you stopped loving her?

PEARCE   No, I did love her but she couldn't believe it.

HOGARTH   Why should she? Why should she have faith
          in you?

PEARCE   Why not? What was there to lose? Nothing.
                But she might have gained something . . .

HOGARTH   Yes, more pain. Good God, she might have
                come to depend on you!

PEARCE   She need not have died alone.

HOGARTH   We all die alone, Doctor. You should know
                that better than any of us.
                Man's terrible pride. His vain desire to
                change human nature! Such arrogance!
                Perhaps God made the world as it should be
                and we should leave well alone. How can we
                hope to improve it?

PEARCE   You don't believe that . . .

HOGARTH   Study history and what do you see? A terrible
                sameness in man's institutions. People are
                greedy and self-seeking . . . I know I am.

PEARCE   I won't believe that, I won't . . .

HOGARTH   You will when the pain gets worse.

PEARCE   What pain?

HOGARTH   Your headaches, Doctor.

PEARCE   They'll soon be gone . . .

HOGARTH   Then you'll despair.

PEARCE   No.

                (*He gathers himself together, tries to be
                positive.*)

                We must not despair. We must he hopeful . . .

HOGARTH   Despair along the way and failure at the end.

PEARCE   What end? You haven't reached the end. You
            don't know where it ends or even if it does
            end.

HOGARTH   Climb down from your pulpit, Doctor.

PEARCE   We dream, we have visions. If your painting
            is a failure it is because it is too earth-bound.

HOGARTH   Bollocks. It's got a sodding angel in it, what
            more do you want? Besides, it's not meant to
            be uplifting. Make you dream of a beautiful,
            blissful after-life. It's meant to make you feel
            bad. Feel guilty so you put your hand in your
            purse and give money to the hospital.

PEARCE   If that is your aim, then I'm sure you will
            succeed admirably.

HOGARTH   What else is there?
            Perhaps if I could paint the heavens, the sea,
            the countryside: something bigger than man,
            then I would. But I can't. I have to record
            what I see; and what I see is poverty,
            homelessness . . . Political corruption, greed.

PEARCE   There's more to life than that.

HOGARTH   Is there? I can't see it.

PEARCE   Yes you can. They are going to the poolside
            in hope - which is a spiritual state.

HOGARTH   It didn't look very spiritual when they were
            trying to tear you apart, Doctor.

PEARCE   Don't reduce. That's the fault of medicine: to
            see man as a machine - the heart a pump;
            tears, even tears, drops of water to keep the
            eyes moist. You must help us to see the whole
            person, body and soul . . .

HOGARTH   What evidence is there that there is anything
            beyond the pain and suffering of this world?

PEARCE   You've created that canvas from nothing. You
                prove that something can come from nothing.

HOGARTH   Riddles and superstition . . .

PEARCE   All right. That moment there. Jane and the
                child. There at the centre, against that
                beautiful sky; Jane and the child; that is the
                soul of your picture.

HOGARTH   Because she knew she was dying, dying
                childless . . .

PEARCE   And because you are childless too?

HOGARTH   Perhaps.

PEARCE   Her spirit lives on there. In your canvas.
                She is remembered . . .

HOGARTH   By us maybe . . .

PEARCE   Yes . . .

HOGARTH   But who will remember us?

PEARCE   Your fame is assured.

HOGARTH   Is it?

PEARCE   Believe me.

HOGARTH   It's not a complete failure?

PEARCE   Far from it.

                (HOGARTH *is going. The light is changing. It
                is mid-way between the chiaroscuro of the
                18th-century scenes and a bright modern
                light.* HOGARTH *withdraws.* PEARCE *stands as
                he did during the Prologue to Act One. He
                seems to be looking at the painting. After a
                moment or two* JANE *comes on. She is, once
                again, entirely a figure from the modern
                world, though recognisably the* JANE *from*

PEARCE'S dream. She carries her briefcase, having come straight from work. She is very pissed off.)

JANE

There you are. I've been looking all over the hospital for you. The bloody traffic. Why couldn't we have met at the Barbican?

(*She kisses him in a perfunctory way. She doesn't notice how distracted PEARCE seems.*)

PEARCE

I wanted . . . see the paintings . . .

JANE

I've seen them before, Danny. Jesus, it's been one problem after another today . . . The printer has put the Asian feature against a shitty brown. I said sort of henna, reddish brown you know. He's chosen shit brown. They'll have to he reprinted. Have you got the tickets?

PEARCE

No. You have.

JANE

Have I?

(JANE *starts to search for them. She doesn't notice that PEARCE appears to be in some distress now.*)

JANE

What's the point of going to fucking Ceylon to shoot the pictures if they end up floating on the top of a cesspool? 'Cos that's what they look like. I said to Max . . .

PEARCE

Sri Lanka.

JANE

. . . looks like they're floating on a cesspool. What?

PEARCE

Fucking Ceylon is fucking Sri Lanka. Has been sincc 1972.

JANE

I know that darling. I spent three weeks there. It's just I prefer 'Ceylon' - as a

concept. Just like I prefer 'Persia'. In fashion
'Persia' is exotic silks, beautiful carpets and
romance. Iran is mad mullahs and women kept
in purdah.

(*She finds the tickets.*)

JANE   Voilà!
                I need a drink.

PEARCE   I don't think I can go, Jane.

JANE   What?

PEARCE   I've got this . . . headache, I feel . . .

JANE   Shit Danny, the tickets cost forty quid.

PEARCE   You go.

JANE   I don't want to go on my own.

PEARCE   Use the phone there in the office. Ask John.

                (*A moment's hesitation.*)

JANE   John is probably on his second bottle of wine
                by now. You're really annoying, d'you know
                that? You and your headaches. You should
                see someone about it.

PEARCE   Yes.

                (JANE *considers.*)

JANE   You're sure you wouldn't mind?

PEARCE   Yes.

JANE   Actually, you do look ghastly. Perhaps we'd
                better both go straight home . . . You're
                sweating.

PEARCE   It's a touch of flu I think.

JANE Well keep away from me, I can't be off work at the moment.

(*Silence.*)

You say there's a phone in there?

PEARCE Yes.

JANE I'll try John.

(JANE *goes off. The Doctors from the opening of Act One begin to reassemble. One of them speaks. They surround* PEARCE *but at no stage do they touch him. It's all happening inside his head. He realises that he is the patient and starts to panic.*)

DOCTOR Today I can promise you something of great interest.
A fellow with a cancerous tumour in the brain.
The skull is a rigid globe that will not permit any expansion from within.
Unless we can reduce the pressure that the growth is creating inside the cranium he is sure to collapse and die.

PEARCE No, no . . . Not me, not me.

(PEARCE *is going into an epileptic fit. He moves his head from side to side.*)

DOCTOR Lay hold of his limbs.
Give him the leather to bite on.
First we cut a flap of scalp that we can peel back to expose the skull. Hold him. Hold him.

(*They've gone by the time that* PEARCE *reaches blindly for the back of the chair.* PEARCE *loses consciousness and falls to the ground with a hoarse cry as air is driven from his chest. His limbs are rigid, the legs*

*extended and the arms flexed. All the muscles
of the trunk and limbs are in strong
contraction simultaneously. The dream figures
withdraw. The convulsions continue.* JANE
*comes back from making her phone call.
When she sees what is happening she doesn't
know what to do.)*

JANE   Danny, Danny. Jesus.
What is it? What's happening . . .

*(*JANE *tries to restrain him. She cannot. She
stands back.* PEARCE'S *generalized
contractions are now interrupted by short
periods of relaxation. Violent jerking of the
muscles at progressively longer intervals.
The jerking stops.* PEARCE *is comatose. His
breathing is harsh. The fit is over. Music.
Lights fade to blackout.)*

End of Act One.

ACT TWO

Music.

The early hours of the morning in Saint Bartholomew's Hospital, where PEARCE *has been admitted. Light comes up on* KATE, *dressed for her work as a Senior Registrar in Neurosurgery.* JANE *waits for her in the shadows.*

KATE   The patient presented with a fit which was witnessed by a doctor who was on the scene before the tonic stage was over.
                The patient was in a coma for approximately twenty minutes.
                On recovery he appeared confused and drowsy. He vomited and complained of a severe headache.
                Upon examination there were signs of venous engorgement of the optic fundi and of papilloedema. We decided that the intracranial pressure was raised and proceeded directly to a head scan.
                The anatomy of the lesion was displayed in some detail.
                We are dealing with a tumour of the left temporal lobe.

                (She falters slightly but then continues in the same matter-of-fact style.)

                Tumours of the temporal lobe may give rise to peculiar interruptions of consciousness - psychic seizures preceded by an aura that resembles dreams . . .

                (She pauses for a moment and breathes deeply to compose herself. KATE *is a friend of* PEARCE'S *and has met his wife on previous occasions. She is dreading what she is about to do. She crosses to* JANE.)

JANE   It's not just epilepsy is it?

KATE   No.

                (*Pause.*)

                The scan shows something in the head.

JANE   Oh God, what?

KATE   A lesion. It could be an infection, it could be
                a tumour.

                (JANE *is trying hard to control her feelings.*)

JANE   Do you mean cancer?

KATE   Not necessarily. But we do need to find out if
                we are to treat it appropriately. We need to
                do a biopsy.

JANE   Oh Jesus, God . . . that's what it is. It's
                cancer.

KATE   There are certain risks.
                Do you want me to go on?

JANE   Yes.

KATE   In order to obtain a sample we would need to
                make a small hole over the tumour and then
                gently insert a needle to collect some tissue.
                Sometimes the needle can provoke a
                haemorrhage . . . There's a chance he may
                be worse afterwards. But there's also the
                opportunity to remove fluid and reduce the
                pressure.

                (JANE *struggles to make sense of* KATE'S
                words.)

JANE   Jesus . . . I feel sick . . .

KATE   I think the risk is justifiable.

                (*Pause.*)

JANE	Can't you just . . . remove it . . . ?
KATE	We'll need to wait for the results of the biopsy.
JANE	Kate . . . ?
KATE	There are problems.
JANE	Yes . . . ?
KATE	Tumours of the nervous system have indistinct boundaries. They are often more extensive than they appear. To rid the patient of the tumour by surgery is to run the risk of unacceptable disability.
JANE	So there's nothing you can do?
KATE	I'm not saying that.
JANE	Then what are you saying?
KATE	One step at time, Jane. The biopsy first. *(Pause.)*
JANE	How could . . . ? *(Silence.)*
KATE	Go on.
JANE	You and Danny are friends . . .
KATE	Yes.
JANE	So how could you? Do that to him? I mean would you be doing it?
KATE	It's my job Jane, it's what I'm trained to do. *(Silence.)*
JANE	Of course. Do what you think best.

(*Pause.*)

KATE   Has he complained of headaches recently?

JANE   No. Not really. Not to me.

KATE   He hasn't reported seeing things, hearing things?

JANE   "Reported"? What makes you think he "reports" to me?

KATE   It's just a phrase, Jane.

JANE   Well they're all just phrases aren't they? "Your husband is going to be all right." "Your husband is going to die." Just phrases.

(JANE *gets up and walks away.* KATE *follows her.*)

JANE   The wonders of modern fucking medicine! Maybe we'd be better off on our knees praying together. Shit. Don't follow me.

(KATE *stops.* JANE *goes in a different direction, crying now.*)

KATE   Where are you going?

(JANE *stops.*)

JANE   I don't know. I don't know where I'm going.

KATE   Jane, come on, sit down.

JANE   I don't want to sit down. I need some fresh air.

KATE   Don't you want to see him?

JANE   I'm going to go home Kate, try to get a few hours sleep before work.

KATE   Work?

JANE   Yes, work.
                          If Danny can't work . . .
                          Get some sleep . . .
                          I'll go in this morning as usual.
                          They mustn't know.

KATE   Why?

JANE   No.
                          No one must know.

KATE   That's impossible, Jane. He has a sister, she'll need to be told.

(JANE, *in this fevered, irrational state, starts to leave again.*)

JANE   There's an entire feature needs reprinting. We're behind as it is.

KATE   If you're going home, at least let me give you something to help you sleep . . .

JANE   No.

KATE   Jane, you're in a state of shock.

JANE   I have to go now.

(JANE *walks off.*)

I have to go.

(KATE *watches her go.*)

KATE   The whole hospital is in a state of shock . . .
A shudder went through the place as staff heard the news.
Fear, tinged with what? A kind of excitement. Not just another admission, clinical, matter-of-fact. But Danny Pearce, a colleague, one of us. Too close for comfort, much too close.

* * * *

(A lighting change. We are in PEARCE'S *room which is softly lit.* PEARCE *is sitting alone in hospital robe and gown.* KATE *comes to him.)*

KATE   How are you feeling?

PEARCE   As if my head is filled with water. If I move it from side to side it rushes back and forth.

KATE   Then don't move it from side to side.
I guess you already know everything you need to know about the op?

PEARCE   Yes.

(Silence. They are very awkward about the new relationship.)

KATE   Danny, about a month ago we had attended a meeting in the Great Hall. As we came out, at the top of the stairs, you paused.

PEARCE   Yes.

KATE   You seemed to be staring at the painting that hangs there . . .
You were pale, mumbling . . . You looked absent - just for a moment.
Then you turned and went back into the Hall - I thought you'd forgotten something.
Was that an attack?

PEARCE   You tell me.

KATE   The first?

PEARCE   Not the first.

KATE   God. And I saw it.
You knew what was happening to you?

PEARCE   Yes.

KATE   Then why didn't you come to see us? You only had to cross the courtyard.

PEARCE	To be told what I already knew?
KATE	You couldn't know. Not for sure.
PEARCE	Maybe not then. But I do now.
KATE	How?
PEARCE	My dream. Tumour in the temporal lobe, malignant and inoperable.
KATE	Even I don't know that much yet. Have you been treating yourself?
PEARCE	For the pain and nausea.
KATE	Danny, I don't understand . . .
PEARCE	I didn't want to be a patient. Hand in your clothes at the door, hand in your name. Obey the rules and regulations. Go to sleep, wake up. Eat now, piss now, shit now. I didn't want that.
KATE	Then don't be . . .
PEARCE	What?
KATE	Once we get you sorted, don't be a patient. Usually in this situation I ask the person if there's anything they've always really wanted to do. If there is, I tell them to go do it.
PEARCE	I've always wanted to be a father and watch my child grow up.

(KATE *turns away.* PEARCE *relents.*)

There is something . . .

KATE	Yes?
PEARCE	You know those weekends you have in Paris?

KATE   Yes.

PEARCE   I've always wanted you to take me with you.

KATE   Now he tells me . . .

PEARCE   You mean it's too late?

KATE   It's just that I think we'd be missed . . .

              (*Silence.*)

PEARCE   Have you ever sat with a dying patient?

KATE   What do you mean?

PEARCE   Sat with someone and watched them die?

KATE   No.

PEARCE   I can remember, when I was a student,
              rushing to look into the eyes of a woman who
              had just died, to see the blood actually
              beginning to break up in the veins of the
              retina.
              I thought it interesting.
              I've been living a lie with Jane. At work . . .
              Recently, when I've picked up a scalpel I've
              felt such a sense of failure.
              It's all been such a failure . . .

              (*Silence.* SIMON, *an orderly, arrives prepared
              to cut a section of* PEARCE'S *hair away.*)

KATE   This is Simon. He's going to cut your hair for
              me. Do you two know each other?

              (PEARCE *cannot help but smile because*
              SIMON *is the* HOGARTH *of* PEARCE'S *dream.*)

PEARCE   We've seen each other around.

KATE   A Nurse will be along to do the pre-med in a
              minute Danny.

(PEARCE *nods.* KATE *is about to leave.*)

PEARCE   Doctor. Good luck.

(KATE *nods, leaves.* PEARCE *turns to* SIMON.)

PEARCE   You know, in Hogarth's time, butchers and
           doctors weren't allowed to sit on juries. It was
           thought that they were too hardened by their
           trades.

SIMON   Are you frightened?

PEARCE   What, about you cutting my hair?
           Yes. I'm frightened.

(SIMON *stands above* PEARCE *in a position
reminiscent of the operation in Act One.*)

SIMON   Here, just relax.

(SIMON *gently soothes* PEARCE'S *forehead.*
PEARCE, *despite everything, closes his eyes
and goes with it as the lights go down on him
and* SIMON.)

                    * * * *

(*A spotlight picks out* KATE. *It is several
hours later and she is exhausted. Perhaps
she's in her green gown from the operating
theatre. At first her voice is flat, almost
expressionless with fatigue.*)

KATE   Reduction of the intracranial pressure was
           achieved by intravenous dehydrating and
           controlled respiration . . . A burr hole was
           made over the tumour and a fragment of
           tissue aspirated into the lumen of a wide bore
           brain needle inserted gently into the tumour.
           The pathologist's report confirmed our
           suspicions: the patient has a glioblastoma
           grade IV - malignant and inoperable . . .

We have begun symptomatic treatment by
steroids.

(*Suddenly her professionalism deserts her.
She all but breaks down.*)

Oh shit. Shit shit shit.

(*She sobs for a moment then regains control.*)

I phoned Danny's sister Ruth and told her.

(KATE *leaves.* RUTH *comes forward.*)

RUTH   I got the first train from Manchester.
            So strange to see people going about their
            lives as if nothing had happened. As if there
            hadn't been this . . . disaster.
            When I arrived at his room the bed was
            empty.
            And for a moment . . . for a moment . . .
            Feel sick . . . sinking feeling . . .
            Stepping into nothing . . . drowning . . .
            I found him at the end of the corridor. Where
            the light through the window made a pool on
            the polished floor.

            (PEARCE *enters into just such a light. He's in
            distress after his operation, confused and
            groggy, sometimes in his dream world,
            sometimes lucid and aware of what's really
            happening around him. A small plaster covers
            the wound.* RUTH *approaches him. She tries
            to get him back to bed, one arm around his
            shoulders. He is trembling, his face wet with
            sweat. He starts to try and remove the
            plaster.*)

RUTH   No, no, leave that now Danny . . .

PEARCE   Too many people, too many . . .

RUTH   Come on Danny, come back to bed . . .

PEARCE   Too many sick . . .

RUTH   Yes.

PEARCE   Can you see them?

RUTH   No my love . . .

PEARCE   Help me.

RUTH   Yes. I'm here to help you. Ruth's here now.

PEARCE   Ruth . . . ?

RUTH   Yes, my love . . .

PEARCE   Your wings are strong and broad . . .

            (*It's as if he's touching wings, out along her arms.*)

            You must trouble the waters.
            Won't you help . . . ?

            (PEARCE *starts to cry. He clings on to her.*)

RUTH   There, there. It's all right . . .

PEARCE   So many dead . . .
            Mum and Dad . . . I tried to help him. His
            silence hurt me. He left me without a word.
            Jane has a lover . . .

RUTH   No Danny . . .

PEARCE   She loves someone else. Someone at the
            office. Not me. John.
            I thought there was a distance between us . . .
            I thought I'd lost my passion for her. But
            when I saw her with that child . . .

RUTH   What child my love?

PEARCE   We'll never have children now will we . . . ?

RUTH   Ssh, ssh, Ruth's here, Ruth's here . . .

PEARCE   I need help myself.

RUTH   Yes . . .

PEARCE   Why me? Why me?
                  I need help myself.

RUTH   I'm here to help you.

PEARCE   You're here aren't you?

RUTH   Yes, I'm here.

PEARCE   My angel.
                  Don't leave me. Help me.

RUTH   I will help you.

PEARCE   Don't leave me . . .

RUTH   I won't . . .

PEARCE   Wrap me in your wings and never leave me.

                  (RUTH *has her arms wrapped around him.*
                  Music as the light fades on them.)

                                  * * * *

                  (JANE *is sitting in* PEARCE'S *room.*)

JANE   Nearly a week, a whole week.
                  Sometimes I go a day keeping the horror just
                  out of sight. I can always glimpse it. It's
                  always there, but by busying myself, by not
                  looking, it can almost be avoided. At the end
                  of the day, I linger until the last person is
                  going home and I have to go. For fear of
                  being alone in the empty office.
                  And outside Covent Garden is buzzing.
                  Young couples, laughing, holding hands,
                  talking to each other about nothing. Flirting.
                  Just hanging around until it can no longer be
                  avoided: the Visit.

The traffic at a standstill, the crush on the
tube, the loonies ranting, the drunks, the
beggars . . .
The hospital reeks of poverty, of failure.
I want to be by a swimming pool, somewhere
in the sun.
Want to be in John's arms again, want to feel
alive . . .
Enough betrayals to last a lifetime . . .

(*The evening light grows to reveal* PEARCE.
Long silence. The atmosphere is very tense.
PEARCE *is bitter, angry at what's happening to
him.*)

PEARCE   I've been planning my funeral.

JANE   What?

PEARCE   Yeah . . .

JANE   Danny, please.

PEARCE   No, it's one of the few consolations. I won't
            have to have a stranger mouthing platitudes
            over my coffin. Some readings, some music.
            It'll be great, I'll be sorry to miss it. I've
            spoken to the chaplain. He says he'll lead a
            secular service. No mention of Heaven or
            God . . .

JANE   You shit.

PEARCE   . . . Good of him, heh?

            (*Silence.* JANE *isn't going to discuss it.*)

PEARCE   Shall I speak to Ruth about it?

JANE   Why not, you speak to her about everything
            else.

            (*Pause.*)

I'm sorry. Sorry sorry sorry sorry sorry.

PEARCE   The whole tone of death is set by the dying
           isn't it? All the misplaced hope, the refusal to
           accept the signs and symptoms. The problem
           is I'm a doctor and I know only too well
           what's happening to me.

           (JANE *can't take this.*)

JANE   I have to go now . . .

PEARCE   Yeah?

JANE   I have some work to do tonight.

           (*Pause. She goes.*)

PEARCE   Running to the arms of her lover.

                          * * * *

           (SIMON *is with* PEARCE *in his room. Lights
           come up on* KATE.)

KATE   In former times we would have spoken of
           Danny being possessed and sent for the
           Priest . . .
           I can record by means of EEG that in addition
           to the occasional 'grand mal' seizures there is
           an almost incessant seething in the temporal
           lobes . . . but that leaves me feeling earth-
           bound and limited - cut off from the real life
           of the mind, the soul.
           His . . . what? . . . visions? . . . have a
           neurological cause, but does that invalidate
           them as visions?
           It's frightening, I look beyond the clinical,
           the mechanical and I find . . . nothing . . .

           (*Light comes up on* PEARCE *and* SIMON.
           Sunlight streams through PEARCE'S *window.*)

PEARCE   I've been trying to write Jane a letter, say
                the things I've failed to say over the years.
                When I look at what I've written it just seems
                bitter and cruel.

                (*Silence.*)

                It's good to have the window. There never
                seemed to be time just to look around in the
                past.
                The sky changes in ways I'd never noticed
                before . . .
                Now I have the time to look, I can't enjoy it.

SIMON   Why can't you?

PEARCE   It's all too late . . .

                (PEARCE *gets out a small piece of paper. He
                hands it to* SIMON.)

PEARCE   Will you read it to me?

SIMON   "Now there is at Jerusalem, by the sheep
                market a pool which is called in the Hebrew
                tongue Bethesda, having five porches.
                In these lay a great multitude of impotent
                folk, of blind, of halt, withered, waiting for
                the movement of the water,
                For an angel went down at a certain season
                into the pool and troubled water: whosoever
                then first after the troubling of the water
                stepped in was made whole of whatsoever
                disease he had.
                And a certain man was there, which had an
                infirmity thirty-and-eight years.
                When Jesus saw him lie, and knew he had
                been now a long time in that case, he saith
                unto him, Wilt thou be made whole?
                The impotent man answered him, Sir, I have
                no man, when the water is troubled, to put me
                into the pool: but while I am coming another
                steppeth down before me.

Jesus saith unto him: Rise, take up thy bed
and walk.
And immediately, the man was made whole,
and took up his bed and walked."

(*Silence.*)

PEARCE   I thought I'd been given that . . . by Hogarth.
           My sister pointed out it's my writing.
           Have you seen the painting?

SIMON   It's the reason I ended up here.

PEARCE   Really?

SIMON   I'd applied to several hospitals. Most were
           more convenient than this place. I came to be
           interviewed. They were restoring the
           paintings at the time.
           I stood and watched.
           I thought then, I think I could work in this
           place. Pity the patients don't see them.

PEARCE   Yes.
           There are so many figures crowding into my
           head.
           Ragged and shuffling. With injuries and
           deformities, all seeking help. Figures from the
           canvases, patients, people I've seen in the
           streets, on the tube . . .
           And the dead - my mother, my father . . .

           (*Silence.*)

SIMON   And Hogarth?

PEARCE   No, it's not the painting or the world of the
           painting any more. The sick are crowding
           under a real sky, in a real landscape. The
           pools are there.

SIMON   Pools?

PEARCE   What?

SIMON   There's more than one?

PEARCE   Yes. A shallow one, with steps, then others
          feeding it, other deeper, darker pools . . .

          (*Silence.*)

SIMON   When did your parents die?

PEARCE   My mother died two years ago. My father in
          1965.

SIMON   How?

PEARCE   He'd fought for the Republicans in Spain.

SIMON   Really?

PEARCE   He'd been a card-carrying communist in his
          youth - left the Party over Hungary. He was
          wounded in Spain . . . I don't know, I think
          he died from those wounds. I suppose in the
          end he just turned his face to the wall.

          (*Pause.*)

          My only legacy is that he taught me the
          French Revolutionary calendar - parrot
          fashion. Vendémaire, Brumaire, Frimaire . . .
          They'd used it in Spain.
          Have you got family?

SIMON   I have a younger sister at university and a
          younger brother who is a ballet dancer in
          Berlin.

PEARCE   Really?

SIMON   Yes. He's the only one who seems to have
          survived my mother's depressions. Or
          escaped them. She's Polish and in mourning
          for her life, like a character from Chekhov.

PEARCE   How is it that you're a porter, Simon?

SIMON   What do you mean?

PEARCE   Well you seem . . .
               How do you get on with the other porters?

SIMON   Fine. I let them put their page-three girls up
               in the locker room, they let me put up my
               quotations from Sartre . . .

PEARCE   Are you taking the piss?

SIMON   It's what your question seemed to deserve.

PEARCE   I didn't mean to offend you.

SIMON   You haven't.

PEARCE   Polish?

SIMON   You can call me Szymon.

PEARCE   Szymon.

               (SIMON *gets up to leave.*)

SIMON   I'd better get on, bedpans to wash.
               Have you tried Polish vodka?

PEARCE   No.

SIMON   I'll bring you some.

               (SIMON *leaves him.* PEARCE *returns to look
               out of the window. Lights fade.*)

                              * * * *

               (*Three pub chairs occupied by* JANE, KATE
               and RUTH. *Light comes up on* JANE.)

JANE   Comic Relief Day. All kinds of stupidity in
               London. Cars with red noses. People in
               clowns outfits collecting in the street . . .

At the centre of it all, the party-pooper. It's as
if I wear a sign saying "No fun in my life.
Talk to me about cancer."
I'm told chemotherapy and radiotherapy can
cure certain cancers. "Yes but not this one".
I'm told pain relief is now so sophisticated he
won't suffer. "But he does suffer."
I'm told about hypnosis, counselling,
herbalism, acupuncture, visualisation. Prayer.
I've joined a club. A club with a huge
membership.
Never discussed before I now find cancer
has touched so many lives. People talk about
their parents, their brothers and sisters . . .
"My son." "My daughter."
"Me."

(*Lights come up on the scene. They're on the
riverside terrace of the Anchor pub. They all
have drinks.* KATE *has just finished a long
stretch of duty at the hospital and is
exhausted.* JANE *is on her lunch hour,* RUTH
has been visiting PEARCE. *It's not really warm
enough to sit outside but* RUTH *insisted.*)

RUTH   I'd like to live near water. The light is quite
            different.
            Look, we could walk along the edge down
            there. I wonder how far you could get?

JANE   It's disgusting, look how muddy it is.

KATE   How's work?

JANE   I get by.

            (*They drink.*)

RUTH   Samuel Pepys is said to have stood on the
            terrace of this pub to watch the Great Fire of
            London.

KATE   Look at it now. A city of cranes.
            St Paul's looks lost.

RUTH   There's a house along there where Wren
            lived during the building of St Pauls . . .

JANE   You sound like a tourist guide.

RUTH   Look to your left, Ladies and Gentlemen and
            you will see a miserable sod.

JANE   Well, what do you expect?

RUTH   That you and I, of all people at the moment,
            should be friends . . .
            You should ease up Jane, on yourself and on
            me.

            (*Silence.*)

KATE   I must get home. I'm shattered.

RUTH   Have another - it'll help you sleep.

            (RUTH *ignores* KATE'S *response and goes off
            to get more drinks. Pause.*)

JANE   How much longer do you think it will go on,
            Kate?

KATE   What?
            Jane, please. It's not the time or the place to
            discuss Danny's illness.

JANE   We talk about little else . . .

KATE   No, I mean if you're asking for a prognosis.
            I shouldn't be here at all really.
            My consultant would have a fit if he knew.
            He thinks I'm too emotionally involved as it
            is.

JANE   I'm the last person to want to talk about it all
            the time . . .

KATE   Yes, you are.

JANE	What does that mean?
KATE	You said it . . .
JANE	But I wasn't saying that was bad . . .
KATE	Nor was I. It would be easier for you if Danny was at home . . .
JANE	Last weekend was a disaster, for both of us. It's just too painful. It was as if he'd never lived there. I was scared all the time, watching him in case he had a seizure. Besides, I'm not going to give up my work. If I lose that I lose everything. It's the only bit of normality left in my life. I'll be no use to Danny then.
KATE	Perhaps Ruth could look after him?
JANE	Yes, she could, but you know Danny doesn't want that.
	(RUTH *returns with drinks. There's an awkward silence.*)
RUTH	Emily has got piano exams tomorrow. I should have sent a card.
KATE	Is she good?
RUTH	No. Hopeless. Like me, all thumbs.
KATE	Have you got a photograph?
RUTH	Yes.
	(*She shows it to* KATE. JANE *is upset.*)
KATE	She's so sweet.
RUTH	She's smiling like that because she's wearing a brace.

KATE   Who's that?

RUTH   Me. It's my spotlight photograph.

KATE   It doesn't look anything like you.

RUTH   I know.

          (*They're laughing. They suddenly notice that*
          JANE *is crying.* RUTH *and* KATE *try to comfort*
          her but JANE *resists.*)

JANE   Look, don't feel sorry for me. I'm not crying
          for Danny. I'm crying for myself. Purely
          selfishly for myself.
          And I am glad I haven't got children and
          probably never will have because I think the
          world is a shitheap and the sooner the
          fucking icecap melts or whatever it is that
          you're always going on about, and we get
          washed away, the better. Because if that can
          happen to Danny . . . then it could happen to
          me . . .

          (*Silence.*)

RUTH   You can cry for yourself sweetheart. It's
          okay.
          Don't be so hard on yourself . . .

JANE   It's all happening too fast for me . . .
          Everything is moving too fast . . .
          When his mother was ill, your mother, Danny
          would undress her and bath her and do her
          hair . . .
          I couldn't . . . I couldn't even find anything to
          say to her.
          It's just the way I am . . .
          I know I'm missing what chances there are of
          making things right . . . I know . . . God, I
          don't know, perhaps it's too late . . .

RUTH   No it's not, love . . .

JANE   Isn't it?

RUTH   No. It's never too late.

                (*Lights fade on* JANE, RUTH *and* KATE.)

                             * * * *

                (*Light comes up on* PEARCE *who is sitting in a
                wheelchair. His right side is beginning to be
                affected by the tumour. His arm is crooked
                and his hand clenched. Without thinking
                about it, he constantly puts his hand back into
                position and uncurls his fingers. Suddenly
                there is mayhem as two Doctors charge in.*
                KATE *is with them.*)

KATE   I'm sorry, they insisted.

1ST DOCTOR   We wanted you to cast your expert eye over
                our act.

PEARCE   Act?

1ST DOCTOR   We're raising money.

                (*They put on red noses.*)

2ND DOCTOR   Where have you been, Danny? Comic relief.

PEARCE   Charity . . . ?

2ND DOCTOR   Now don't start getting political on us. We're
                performing tonight.

1ST DOCTOR   At this very moment fifteen students are
                streaking across Blackfriars Bridge.

2ND DOCTOR   Shit, you're joking? I wanted to see that. I
                heard Jenny's going to do it.

1ST DOCTOR   Oh Danny, you remember Jenny . . .

KATE   Come on now. I told you not to be too long
                about it.

1ST DOCTOR   Okay. Okay.

(*The Doctors put on their dark glasses,
remove their red noses and sing in harmony,
"You've Lost that Loving Feeling". Silence.
Awkwardness. In their way, they obviously
intended some tribute to* PEARCE.)

PEARCE   Not very funny . . .

1ST DOCTOR   Not even if we wear the noses?

               (*A few bars of a horrid, exaggerated nasal
               version.* KATE'S *seen enough.*)

KATE   Okay. Let the man rest now . . .

2ND DOCTOR   Sorry you can't be there Danny, we'll be
               thinking of you.

               (PEARCE *nods.* KATE *and the* 2ND DOCTOR
               leave. The 1ST DOCTOR *can't find any words
               to express his sorrow. He leaves.* PEARCE
               turns away to his window. As he does so,
               SIMON *enters.*)

PEARCE   What do you want?

               (SIMON *pulls a bottle of flavoured Polish
               vodka from his coat pocket.*)

SIMON   Vodka. Flavoured with Zubrowka, the
               fragrant herb beloved by the European
               Bison.

PEARCE   Look. I'm in pain. I'm sick every fifteen
               minutes, my eyesight's bad and everything
               seems dull and grey and shitty and fucking
               bleak. All right?

SIMON   Is that a no?
               You don't mind if I do?

PEARCE   Do what you like, it's you they'll sack.
               At least they came to see me I suppose.
               Usually the medical staff do what they can to
               avoid the terminally ill.

SIMON	I'm not surprised if they're all as hopeless as you.

(SIMON *fills his glass and knocks it straight back.*)

Na Zdrowie!

PEARCE	What have I got to he hopeful about?

Hope the pain doesn't get worse, hope the end comes quickly, hope Jane will be all right?
That's not hope. That's fear. I'm afraid of the pain. I'm afraid of the end. I'm afraid for Jane. Fear, not hope . . .

(SIMON *pours himself another. Drinks it in silence.*)

There's nothing without hope . . .

SIMON	Bullshit. There's nothing without love and you have Jane . . .
PEARCE	Do I?
SIMON	. . . and you have Ruth.

(SIMON *pours himself a third. He coaxes* PEARCE.)

Mmm. Remarkably full. Vanilla-like palate. Gently herbal and soothing.

PEARCE	Jesus, pour us a fucking glass then.

(*He pours.*)

SIMON	Down in one.
PEARCE	I won't taste it.
SIMON	You'll taste it.

(*Na Zdrowie!*)

PEARCE   You're right. Cold and hot at once. Quite a
                cocktail given the drugs I'm on.

SIMON   I first had this one last summer at my Great
                Aunt's in Warsaw. I made the mistake of
                calling it Zubrovka, which is the Russian
                version.

PEARCE   She doesn't like Russian vodka?

SIMON   She doesn't like Russians. She too is in
                mourning - for the loss of the family estate in
                Lvov. It's now a rehabilitation centre for drug
                addicts.

                (*He pours two more shots of vodka.*)

                By Polish standards she's quite wealthy too.
                When they fled the advancing Russians, she
                swallowed as many of the family jewels as she
                could. Whenever I see her, so refined and
                proper, I have this mental image of her
                picking diamonds out of her shit. She can't
                face her past, she can't forgive, she can't
                forget.

                (PEARCE *is grimacing. He rests his eyes.*)

SIMON   Are you in pain?

PEARCE   Constantly.

SIMON   Do you want me to call a nurse?

PEARCE   No.

SIMON   Would you like to listen to some music? I can
                lend you my . . .

PEARCE   You are a true believer aren't you?

SIMON   In?

PEARCE   The distractions of art.
                Pearce is feeling sorry for himself, play him
                some Handel.

SIMON	Not as a distraction.
PEARCE	What then?
SIMON	More than that.
PEARCE	What? Go on.
SIMON	If I'm down it lifts my spirits.
PEARCE	I'm not "down" Simon, I'm dying.
SIMON	I'm sick of this. There are the live and there are the dead. You my friend are alive and the sooner you face up to that the better.
PEARCE	Fuck you. I know what you're doing. With your stories. Your brother in Berlin. Your family in Poland . . .
SIMON	Do you?
PEARCE	Making sure I don't get too self-centred, begin to think in my illness that the world revolves around me . . . Well? Am I right?
SIMON	No you're not.
PEARCE	Then why?
SIMON	Because I . . . like you . . .
PEARCE	Jesus, I thought you were going to say "love you" then . . .
SIMON	Because I love you.

(*This is hard for* PEARCE *to take. Far from softening he gets harsher.*)

PEARCE	You don't fucking know me.

SIMON   Better than you think, perhaps.

PEARCE   Fuck you. Go and raise someone else's
          consciousness.
          I don't need your pity.
          Perhaps I'm one of those poor sods for
          whom disease brings nothing but pain and
          humiliation.

          (PEARCE *starts to lose his breath*.)

SIMON   Yeah?

PEARCE   No catharsis, no spiritual growth . . .
          Just a bitch from beginning to end . . .
          I know what my hallucinations were telling
          me.
          Stop playing Christ, deciding people's futures.
          You can't heal anyone, you can't even heal
          yourself . . .

SIMON   Have faith in your demons, Danny.
          Perhaps Jesus was part of your dream
          because you feel the need to love.

          (PEARCE *throws his vodka into* SIMON'S *face.*
          SIMON *stares at him*.)

PEARCE   What's this? Turn the other cheek?
          Why don't you hit me? Go on, hit me.
          Oh, fuck off, you Polack bastard.

          (SIMON *turns and leaves.* PEARCE *remains,
          tight mouthed, stubborn. After a while he
          gives way to his emotion*.)

PEARCE   (*quietly*) I'm sorry, Simon, I'm sorry . . .

          (*Music as lights dim in* PEARCE'S *room*.)

                    * * * *

          (PEARCE *is in his wheelchair. Light comes up
          on* JANE.)

JANE   So many memories . . .
              In bed one night, when the planning for the
              trip to Sri Lanka was getting me down and I
              couldn't sleep, Danny invented the alphabet
              game . . .
              I had to say a word, or phrase, for each letter
              in turn.
              Just let the word come to me, a sort of
              exorcism I suppose. And I remember
              gradually being able to laugh at the things
              that were troubling me:
              Art directors that don't listen; bags waiting to
              be packed; clothes still not finished; delays at
              the airports . . .
              Alone in bed last night, I played the game
              again:
              Anger; Bitterness; Cancer; Death . . .

              (*Lights come up on* PEARCE *as well. They're
              in the hospital grounds.* JANE *is pushing*
              PEARCE *in a wheelchair. They come to rest.*)

JANE   Is this all right?

PEARCE   Yeah. Look how fast the clouds are moving.
              It seems as though the world's on fast
              forward.
              Or is it just me?

              (*He looks at* JANE. *She's not really listening.*)

              I've never been able to imagine living in the
              twenty-first century. The idea of the year
              2000 has always filled me with dread.

              (*Pause.* PEARCE *looks in* JANE'S *eyes.*)

              Do you still see John?

JANE   What?

PEARCE   Are you seeing John?

JANE   I see him at work . . .

PEARCE   You know what I mean.
                Are you sleeping with him?

JANE   No, I'm not sleeping with him.
                Or anyone else.

PEARCE   But you were?

                (*She can't deny it.*)

                How long for?

JANE   Four months.

                (PEARCE *looks away.* JANE *moves from him.*)

PEARCE   You haven't since I've been ill?

JANE   No.

                (*Silence.*)

PEARCE   Tell me why.

JANE   Danny, please, I . . .

PEARCE   I want to know why.

JANE   I don't want to talk about it.
                You know why.

                (*Silence. It's true, he does.*)

PEARCE   Were you going to tell me?

JANE   What do you want me to say?

PEARCE   Tell me the truth.

JANE   I hadn't planned to, no.
                It didn't feel like that.

PEARCE   What did it 'feel' like . . . ?

JANE	Separate from us. I suppose because we weren't making love . . .
PEARCE	That wasn't just down to me . . .
JANE	No, of course not . . . I'm not saying I wouldn't have told you. But you didn't ask.
PEARCE	Did you want me to?
JANE	Yes. I did. You should have known.
PEARCE	In a way I did.

(*Silence. But he can't let it go yet.*)

PEARCE	Where?
JANE	What?
PEARCE	Where did you do it?
JANE	Please . . .
PEARCE	Where?
JANE	At his flat.
PEARCE	Not at ours?
JANE	No.
PEARCE	When I was on nights?

(*The answer is "yes". PEARCE is agonized by the thought.*)

JANE	I was using him, Danny. I needed something I wasn't getting from you.
PEARCE	Why didn't you talk to me about it?

JANE   I tried!
                I tried but you were always too tired, or got
                upset so quickly.

PEARCE   I was ill.

JANE   Before that.
                On that awful holiday in Tunisia, I tried then.
                If I'd have known it would have been
                different . . .
                It all seemed harmless. Meaningless really.

PEARCE   Don't deny him for my sake.

JANE   Not meaningless but . . .
                Danny I don't understand why you're doing
                this.

                (PEARCE *is thoughtful*.)

PEARCE   If I can stop hurting myself maybe I can stop
                hurting others.
                I've been as afraid of living as I am of dying.
                I don't want to feel angry any more.
                I want to clear the air.

                (*Pause*.)

JANE   I know I disappoint you. I've let you down,
                I know.
                Not just over John, but your illness too.
                I can go so far and then, I don't know why, I
                have to . . .
                I can't go any further. I can't cope until I've
                had a break from it. I've always been like
                that.
                But I always come back for more.
                Ruth's there all the time for you . . .

PEARCE   I don't want Ruth . . .

JANE   . . . I can't do that.

PEARCE   I want you.

JANE	Do you? Do you really?
	(*Pause.*)
JANE	Oh Danny, I'm not good like you . . .
PEARCE	I'm not good.
JANE	Well you seem it to me.
	(JANE *doesn't notice that they are being approached by a Young Girl in a blue dress.*)
PEARCE	God, we're strangers to ourselves let alone one another . . .
GIRL	Excuse me.
	(JANE *looks up.*)
GIRL	I asked after the doctor. One of the nurses told me he was out here.
JANE	Yes?
GIRL	He treated me. Last November.
PEARCE	Yes, I remember. Sally?
SALLY	Yes.
	(SALLY *approaches him.*)
SALLY	I came for a scan today, asked after you. They told me you were ill . . . That you were out here in the gardens.
PEARCE	How was the scan?
SALLY	All clear.
PEARCE	Good.
SALLY	It suddenly seems a very beautiful day . . .

I hope I'm not being selfish, but I wanted to thank you. I won't forget you.
That sounded awful.

(*She is about to go, when she stops and kisses him spontaneously. She goes, quickly.*)

PEARCE   God. A young girl in a blue dress.

JANE   It seemed to get brighter when she was here.

PEARCE   Yes it did.

(PEARCE *laughs quietly to himself.* JANE *smiles. She laughs too. Suddenly she realises his laughter has turned to tears. She kisses him. Again and again, passionately.*)

JANE   My love, my love.

(*He holds her hands.*)

PEARCE   Do you remember that time we made love at a wedding?

JANE   My cousin's, yes.

PEARCE   Went into the woods and made love.

JANE   Yes.

PEARCE   Afterwards, you wouldn't let me get dressed.

JANE   You looked so lovely . . .

PEARCE   Well the horseflies certainly thought so . . .

JANE   Oh God, yes, you were covered in bites . . .

PEARCE   Thirty-four. I counted them that night.

JANE   To punish me because you'd been on top.

(*Pause. He's looking into her eyes.*)

JANE   What?

PEARCE   I'll always remember the first time I saw you.
              Your eyes.
              It hasn't all been a waste of time has it?

JANE   No my love. Not at all.

              (*Silence.*)

PEARCE   Will you take another lover when I'm dead?

JANE   No . . .

PEARCE   Will you?
              Will you?

JANE   One day. I suppose I will.

PEARCE   Yes. Life goes on . . .

JANE   Does it?

PEARCE   Yes. You should have children too . . .

JANE   Oh don't. Please.

              (*She wipes away his tears.*)

              I'd better take you in, before the wind makes
              your face sore.

              (*Lights go down on* PEARCE *and* JANE.)

                              * * * *

              (*Light comes up on* KATE.)

KATE   The patient has complained of brief attacks of
              darkened vision precipitated by moving or
              stooping.

              (*Lights come up on* PEARCE'S *room as* KATE
              goes. PEARCE *is in his wheelchair.* SIMON *is
              with him.*)

PEARCE   One winter when the weather was very bad
           and I suppose there was no work on the
           building, he took me swimming - to the local
           baths.
           My father had never done that before . . .
           We couldn't believe it when we walked
           round the edge to the cubicles because there
           was steam coming off the surface of the
           water. We got changed and went down the
           steps into the pool, I think we were the only
           two there . . . the water was hot. We just
           drifted in silence. It was too warm to swim.
           I went back to that pool lots of times on my
           own but it was never hot again. I guess the
           boilers must have gone wrong and over-
           heated the water that day. In fact, it was
           always freezing.
           That's the only fond memory of my father that
           I have.
           It must have been that summer that he died.
           He was a sad man. His pain was like a cloud
           over my childhood. Though I understand him
           better now.
           So many memories. It seems we forget
           nothing.

           (*Silence.*)

SIMON   Do you want to try this?

PEARCE   What is it?

SIMON   Cytrynowka. Lemon vodka.

PEARCE   I've had that.

SIMON   No. You've had Wisniowka which is cherry
           and Pieprzowka which is red pepper.

PEARCE   No wonder I have such appalling headaches.
           Oh well. Live dangerously.

SIMON   That's what it's all about.

(*He pours.*)

PEARCE   What do you think, really?

SIMON   . . . ?

PEARCE   What do you think it's all about really?
                What makes life worth living?

SIMON   For me?
                To love and be loved.
                For some people it can be work . . .

PEARCE   And the ability to be alone . . . ?

SIMON   That's being able to love yourself.

                (*They hold up their glasses.*)

SIMON
PEARCE }   Na Zdrowie!

                (*They down it in one.* PEARCE *is sick.* SIMON
                comforts him but no comment is passed.)

PEARCE   I never liked my own company before but I
                crave it now.
                People aren't crowding my head in the same
                way.
                There's sky and sun and the scent of
                heliotrope . . .

SIMON   Do they do package tours to this place?

PEARCE   Club Dead?

                (*They start laughing together.*)

SIMON   I attended a faith healing meeting once. The
                healer, a charismatic man in a white suit,
                called for anyone with an affliction to come
                up.

The first was a man on crutches, one leg
horribly withered . . . the healer said, "what
is your name?"
And the man replied "Frank" and the healer
said, (SIMON *puts his hand on* PEARCE'S
forehead, like a faith healer.) "Do you have
faith Frank?"
Frank said "yes" and the healer said, "go
behind that screen Frank, and pray."
The second person to come up had a terrible
speech impediment but he managed to get out
that his name was John and the healer said,
"Do you have faith John?" and John nodded
and the healer said, "go behind the screen
and pray."
So John went behind the screen with Frank
and they prayed and we all prayed and then
the healer called "Frank, throw down your
crutches and walk. John, speak to us!"
John was the first to emerge and the healer
said, "Speak to us John, speak to us!" and
John said, (*The speech impediment intact*.)
"Frank's fallen over . . . "

(SIMON *and* PEARCE *find this hugely funny,
much funnier than it is. They are still giggling
hysterically with each other when* RUTH
arrives. They try to stop.)

RUTH   It can't have been that funny.

PEARCE   No, it wasn't really.

            (*They struggle to control themselves.* SIMON
            is leaving.)

            Simon.

SIMON   Yes?

PEARCE   Thank you for your Slavic spirit.

            (SIMON *goes*.)

PEARCE Jesus. My head hurts.

RUTH I'm not surprised.

(They laugh together. Pause.)

PEARCE Ruth, I think you should go back to Manchester . . .

RUTH Why?

PEARCE Just for the weekend.

RUTH I don't want to leave you . . .

PEARCE Emily must be missing you . . .

RUTH Don't try to make me feel guilty . . .

PEARCE I'm not, but you mustn't use me . . .

RUTH What do you mean by that?

PEARCE Perhaps you've needed to get away from Joe, from work . . .

RUTH Or the lack of it.

PEARCE Same thing. Jane said you'd turned down a job.

RUTH Yeah. A voice-over . . .

PEARCE Even so . . .

RUTH For fabric softener.

(They laugh.)

PEARCE From Emily even . . . ?

RUTH Are you trying to hurt my feelings?

PEARCE   No. But Emily comes first. She needs you more than I do. You need to care for Emily, after all, she's the closest to a daughter I've got.

RUTH   You think I'm a bad mother?

PEARCE   No, of course not.

RUTH   Anyway, since when have you been so fucking perceptive?

          (*Pause.*)

          All right. But only for the weekend.

PEARCE   Fine. A break from this will do you good.

          (*Pause.*)

          When all this is over . . .

RUTH   Oh don't . . .

PEARCE   When all this is over, I think you should try to find some time to be alone for a while. It's the hardest thing, I know, but your first responsibility is to yourself . . . Not to Joe, or Emily, or me. Not to the planet . . .

RUTH   Don't mock me . . .

PEARCE   All right. But to yourself first, then the planet. There is something you can do for me.

RUTH   Oh is there?

PEARCE   I haven't got any clothes for the summer. Would you buy me some?

RUTH   Yes, of course I will my love.

PEARCE   I'd really like a straw hat.

RUTH   An Italian straw hat.

            (RUTH *is about to go*.)

PEARCE   Don't I get a kiss?

RUTH   I'm not sure whether you deserve one.

            (RUTH *returns and kisses him. She leaves.*
            Music as lights go down on PEARCE.)

                        * * * *

            (*A spotlight comes up on* KATE.)

KATE   In the last week the visions came more often,
            grew deeper, began to occupy most of his
            day.
            The patient, looked rapt, as if in a trance.
            Talked to, he responded clearly, but even
            the most down-to-earth staff talked about him
            being in another world . . .

            (*Music. Moonlight up on* PEARCE'S *room.*
            PEARCE *is sitting in his wheelchair.* KATE
            joins him.)

PEARCE   Vendémaire: the month of vintage.
            Brumaire: the month of fog.

            (KATE *sees* PEARCE *sitting there in the*
            darkness talking to himself. She approaches
            him slowly.)

PEARCE   Frimaire: the month of frost.

KATE   Danny?
            Danny?

            (KATE *is very gentle, recognising* PEARCE *to*
            be partly at least in a world of his own. It is
            as if PEARCE *is meditating, reciting a mantra.*)

PEARCE   Nivôse: the month of snow.

Pluviôse: the month of rain.
Ventôse: the month of wind.
Germinal: the month of germination.
Floréal: the month of flowering.
Prairial: the month of meadows.
Messidor: the month of harvest.
Thermidor: the month of heat.
Fructidor: the month of fruit.

(*Silence.*)

This month is . . . Floréal.

(*Silence. He's about to start again.*)

KATE   What is that?

PEARCE   What?

KATE   You were reciting. Like a prayer.

PEARCE   The French Revolutionary calendar.
              Year One. A new beginning . . .

              (*Silence.*)

KATE   I wanted to tell you. I remembered that I've
              been to Bethesda.

PEARCE   What?

KATE   As a student, I did my elective in Israel.
              I went to Bethesda. "The House of Mercy" in
              Jerusalem.
              It's in the Muslim quarter of the city, looked
              after by the White Fathers.
              There are pools about forty foot deep, too
              deep for the sick. But they excavated and
              found several small basins, some with stone
              steps leading into them, which must have
              been the healing pools. When the small pools
              dried up they would be replenished from the
              deeper ones.

              (KATE *suddenly realises that* PEARCE'S *sight
              has gone.*)

I suppose the fresh water rushing in would make waves.

PEARCE   Yes.

(*Gently she places her hand over his eyes.*)

Yes. "Total eclipse, no sun, no moon . . . "

(*He takes her hand and arm.*)

PEARCE   Such soft flesh, smooth skin.
You know I had the dirtiest Hogarthian dreams about you.

KATE   Really?

PEARCE   Oh yes . . .
All those figures that crowded the canvas, crowded my head - they've all gone now.
I'm alone. Just me and the pool of Bethesda.
I think the soul dies before the body. The body may linger on but the soul cannot take such punishment.
You see it. You see a moment when the spirit departs.
What remains after that is already dead in a way.

(*Pause.*)

PEARCE   Ruth's away this weekend. Can you phone Jane and tell her?

KATE   Of course.

PEARCE   Leave it about an hour.

KATE   All right.

(*She's leaving him.*)

PEARCE   And Kate . . .

KATE   Yes?

PEARCE   Stop my medication.

KATE   Right.

                (*Again* KATE *starts to leave.*)

PEARCE   Kate . . .

KATE   What now?

PEARCE   I do love you. Go easy on yourself.

                (*She has no answer. She leaves him. Music.*
                PEARCE *sees the pool shimmering in front of*
                him.)

                There are deep pools there, so deep, so
                pure . . .
                That all pain passes away, so deep and cool . . .
                Alone now. No body. No body.
                I'll slip into the deep pool and it will be
                finished.
                The silence . . .
                My voice is running away with the sound of
                gushing water . . . Sshhh . . .

                (*Lights down on* PEARCE. *Music continues.*)

                              * * * *

                (*When the light comes up on* JANE, KATE *and*
                RUTH, PEARCE *has gone.*)

JANE   Kate phoned me. By the time I got to the
                hospital Danny was sleeping.

KATE   Towards the end the patient no longer
                responded to external stimuli.

JANE   I sat beside you, took your hand. I love you
                Danny. I won't leave you again.
                Don't worry about me. I'm going to be all
                right.

(JANE *and* KATE *are joined by* RUTH.)

RUTH I was in Manchester. Jane rang to tell me he was not expected to last the night. I was so angry. Why had I left him at all? Did he want me gone? I got a taxi to drive me to London. We hit the morning traffic.
I wished the rest of humanity washed away. Didn't they realise? Why didn't they care?
I made the driver stop and I ran the rest of the way. It was raining and I'd forgotten my coat. My shoes weren't made for running. I slipped, fell over, hurt my knee and suddenly I was eight years old, crying in the street, wanting Danny to come and pick me up, carry me indoors.
But I picked myself up and made the rest of the journey barefoot. When I got there they were so close together, I felt I was intruding, but Jane held out her hand to me.

(*Music. A bow dragged across strings, like dying breaths.*)

JANE His breathing . . .

RUTH Yes . . .

JANE His breath . . .

RUTH Was like the sea dragging the shingle back and forth. It was so hot in the ward. He was sweating.

JANE Sometimes he squeezes my fingers. Do you think he knows I'm here?

KATE Would you like me to give him anything to ease him on his way?

JANE Oh yes, please do.

KATE I did. When I returned later his breath was still laboured. I gave him another injection.

RUTH   Still it went on . . .

KATE   A third time.

                (*The breathing music stops.*)

JANE   His eyes were slightly open. I closed them
                with my fingertips.

RUTH   We clung to each other.

KATE   I watched them, his wife, his sister. They
                looked as if they were behind glass. Like fish
                in a tank. Their mouths opened and closed
                silently. My white coat felt crisp with starch
                and I knew that if I moved it would break the
                silence in the room like a scream.

RUTH   They gave us tea.

JANE   They gave us tea.
                When we went back his face had been
                washed.
                I was stunned. He looked beautiful. Peaceful.

RUTH   We sat with him for a while.
                Neither of us really knew what to do.
                Suddenly I found myself saying a prayer.

JANE   I collected up his things from around the
                room. The books, the cards, the letters.

RUTH   They put screens round the bed and a man
                came with a trolley thing . . .
                We went home.

* * * *

EPILOGUE

Like the Prologue it is one year later. JANE *has the bunch of
red roses she had in the Prologue,* RUTH *her simple bunch
of flowers from the garden.* KATE *is at work.*

KATE   Doctor Daniel Pearce. Male, aged thirty-five
              years, three months: headaches; epilepsy;
              papilloedema; terminal attacks of opisthotonos . . .
              I can't go today, too much work . . .

              (KATE *leaves*.)

JANE   Oh Danny.
              You're a bastard. To leave me like that.
              A year. One year.

RUTH   I went to Kerry. Beneath the mountains,
              beside the ocean. So many memories came
              flooding back.

JANE   I still see you. Sitting in the chair watching
              me. Standing in the bedroom.

RUTH   It's the hardest thing, being alone.
              But bit by bit I began to quite like myself
              again.
              Emily gave me the flowers for your grave.
              She grew them herself from seed . . .

              (RUTH *leaves*. JANE *is alone. Music*.)

JANE   I have taken a lover on occasions.
              But always, during those hours before dawn,
              I've listened to the rhythm of his breathing,
              and when I've stretched out my hand have
              known it was your heart that I felt beating
              beneath the chest where my palm rested.

              (*Music continues as the lights slowly fade to
              blackout*.)